Additional Works by Robert L. Dilenschneider

Power and Influence: The Rules Have Changed (2007)

A Time for Heroes: Business Leaders, Politicians, and Other Notables Explore the Nature of Heroism (2005)

The Corporate Communications Bible: Everything You Need to Know to Become a Public Relations Expert (2004)

50 Plus!: Critical Career Decisions for the Rest of Your Life (2004)

The Critical 2nd Phase of Your Professional Life: Keys to Success for Age 40 and Beyond (2003)

Moses, CEO: Lessons in Leadership (1999)

The Critical 14 Years of Your Professional Life (1998)

The Dartnell Public Relations Handbook (1998 & 1990)

On Power (1994)

A Briefing for Leaders: Communication as the Ultimate Exercise of Power (1992)

Power and Influence: Mastering the Art of Persuasion (1991)

THE AMA HANDBOOK OF PUBLIC RELATIONS

THE AMA HANDBOOK OF PUBLIC RELATIONS

ROBERT L. DILENSCHNEIDER

Foreword by Maria Bartiromo

HarperCollins Leadership

An Imprint of HarperCollins

The AMA Handbook of Public Relations

Published by HarperCollins Leadership, an imprint of HarperCollins Focus LLC.

ISBN 978-0-8144-1525-2 (HC)
ISBN 978-1-4002-4592-5 (paperback)

For **Joan Avagliano,** clearly responsible for my success and one who has taught me much about life. Joan knows better than most why this book is important.

CONTENTS

SECTION THREE

THE BROADER PR SPECTRUM

SECTION FOUR

MAKING IT HAPPEN

FOREWORD

WHEN I WAS A ROOKIE television reporter covering the business beat, my time on air was almost always short. Back then, business news was considered hopelessly boring, and the stations covered it with a grudging sense of duty. The only instructions directors often gave me was: "Just tell us how the Dow Jones did and get off."

How the world has changed! The news cycle is 24/7, and people get their information from a dazzling variety of sources. As for business coverage, it's major news, and "how the Dow Jones did" is often the lead story. This was true even when the U.S. economy was healthy and unemployment low. With the nation and most of the rest of the world in the grip of a severe recession, the fate of markets, the fortunes of banks, and the decisions of CEOs are the subject of wall-to-wall coverage.

In this supercharged environment, knowing how to communicate effectively has become crucially important—more so than ever before. To get ahead, and stay ahead, you must know how to get your message out into the highly competitive marketplace of ideas. You must do it in ways that are clear and consistent. And you must capture and hold the attention of people who are in danger of being swamped by information overload. To achieve all these aims, you need to master an array of communication technologies, both those already in use and new technologies that keep coming on line at an astonishing pace.

Information moves around the world instantly now, and people are shrewder about consuming it. Smart communicators shape their messages to reflect these facts, knowing that openness, directness, and transparency are the qualities that earn respect and build trust.

The best communicators make people feel that the message is meant for them and that the communicator "gets" what it is they care about. It's the ability to touch hearts as well as minds.

Robert Dilenschneider is a master of the art of communicating. Even more important, he is a master of *teaching* the art of communications. In a world where the buzz and chatter can be deafening, he knows how to quietly command the attention of exactly the right audiences.

Sometimes his counsel is wonderfully simple and direct—*know your message and stick to it.* Other times it is subtle and complex, making use of everything from handwritten personal notes to strategically planned dinner engagements. He has that rare gift of connecting with people, whether it's the CEO of a global corporation or the folks who buy the corporation's product.

The AMA Handbook of Public Relations is an operator's manual, a guidebook for communicating in the twenty-first century. The book is a direct reflection of how dramatically the world has changed in the last ten years. It's all about the sophisticated strategies that modern communicators must command if they want to keep ahead.

You'll find plenty of old-school savvy here, too. Some truths never change. But fresh developments keep coming along, and a new synthesis must constantly be created. That is the essence of this book.

In a world that seems to move at warp speed, another edition may be necessary a few years from now. But for today, and for as long as we can see into the future, this is the best communications guide you are going to find. Read it, and use it well.

—Maria Bartiromo

ACKNOWLEDGMENTS

THIS BOOK WOULD NOT HAVE been possible without relying on many to create a useful, broad-ranging, up-to-date, and authoritative book of this nature. To that end, I have cited a series of experts and authorities whose published works on the digital revolution, particularly, provided me with countless valuable insights and recommendations. I have also tapped into the expertise and knowledge of many of my colleagues at The Dilenschneider Group to whom I am indebted. To all, I am very grateful for their sage advice. I would particularly like to thank Joel Pomerantz, Jonathan Zimmerman, and Joan Avagliano for the many hours they spent working with me on the project. Mary Jane Genova helped research many of the major topics within this handbook.

Critical to the success of this writing experience was Edward Reilly, President of the American Management Association, who introduced me to his fine colleagues Hank Kennedy, Ellen Kadin, Barry Richardson, and Erika Spelman. This book would not have been possible without them.

Throughout my career, my wife, Jan, has shown unwavering support and patience. She has stood beside me at every turn and provides me the inspiration in all my endeavors. In this particular volume, my sons, Geoffrey and Peter, helped guide my understanding of the constantly evolving digital revolution that is at the core of this handbook, and I am very grateful to both of them.

THE AMA HANDBOOK OF PUBLIC RELATIONS

INTRODUCTION

"The old paradigms were breaking down faster than the new ones emerging, producing panic among those most invested in the status quo."

—MIT media professor **Henry Jenkins** in *Convergence Culture: When Old and New Media Collide* (New York University Press, 2006)

SUCCESS IN PUBLIC RELATIONS depends on the ability to communicate—to put your ideas and thoughts across to others, to make them listen, to get them to act. And communication now depends on technology that is changing every day.

Public relations was one of the first industries to recognize and harness the power of the Internet. The Web was a natural venue for corporate communications, establishing brands, spreading product information, and much more. PR professionals with vision and imagination jumped on board as soon as they recognized the unparalleled possibilities. But the Internet can also be filled with unexpected dangers and quick-strike ambushes for those who aren't properly prepared.

The AMA Handbook of Public Relations has been written to help you combine traditional media and Web-based campaigns in successfully getting your message out, while at the same time protecting your clients, your company, and yourself against harmful cyberattacks.

Here I am sitting in my office in Manhattan. But I could be sitting in an office just like this one in Algiers, London, Oslo, Beijing, Buenos Aires, Mexico City, Paris, or Calcutta. The reality of technology is the same around the globe.

We in business are trying to figure out how to be successful in a very different century. The key to this is finding out how to exploit the power of the Internet. We know it's there. After all, when Google Inc. speaks, the world listens. Insurance companies, Wall Street, retailers, universities, and industrial companies around the globe know this and are struggling with what to do. This handbook is about how you can gain advantage and bring your skills to a new level and in a new way that will enable you to communicate your message even more effectively in a digital age.

Yet the Internet can be a double-edged sword. You may have been blindsided already by the digital guerilla attacks cyberspace makes possible on reputations, products, and services—and ultimately profits. Three renegades on Twitter.com caused Johnson & Johnson to discontinue its Motrin commercial and issue a mea culpa. The national pizza chain Domino's was victimized by two prankster employees who posted a clip on YouTube of a third employee doing gross things with the food he was preparing. In no time the offensive clip went viral, attracting millions of viewers.

Today is very different from those confident days when public relations agencies executed proven formulas to promote our messages, manage rumors, enhance brands, or support clients during litigation. Every day I get a call from a CEO who asks about something that has happened online and what to do about it. The public relations practitioner must always keep in mind that the Internet—where information travels at warp speed—can be a source of PR nightmares.

On the other hand, the Internet also has helped many people and organizations succeed beyond their wildest dreams. Consider how Senator Barack Obama used technology to reach the White House. Obama is the first president to have weekly Internet chats with the people. Life has changed. CEOs now use the Web to reach managers. Many CEOs are starting to blog. Think about how big corporations are using tech to advance their interests, and how technology has leveled the playing field so that success is not based on who you know, where you're from, or what school you attended, but on what you know about using the new tools available to you.

When I leave this office based over Grand Central Station and take the Metro North commuter train home to Darien, Connecticut, I encounter another aspect of this new reality. Darien, like much of the New York Metro area, still enjoys affluence, but now has a different tone—it has become a community with many unemployed financial markets experts, C-suite executives, and recent graduates from college and professional schools. The jobs they lost, and the ones they were educated for, no longer exist.

To make a living again, they have to reinvent themselves using the Internet and then present their new selves in digital ways. For the lion's share that is a paradigm shift. Most businesspeople are so preoccupied with their careers or schooling that they are behind the learning curve about how to use the Internet as an extension of themselves. That has to change if they are to be successful.

Your world is very different today than it was five years ago, and it will change even more in the next few years. That is what this book is about—helping you to adjust to a new world and to position yourself for what is ahead. If you do not adapt to what has taken place and what is yet to come, you will fall behind; and in a time of economic challenge, that is simply unacceptable.

Adapting may be hard, especially if you've been doing things the same way for years, but you must do it to survive and prosper. Many people over forty are still not completely comfortable with technology. People under forty learned how to use technology early on, but they aren't always adept at using it for business purposes.

Moving to new, or digital, media isn't just a case of transplanting old media. It also involves a new vocabulary, altered interaction with an audience that can now literally talk back, and different standards about objectivity, relevance, and timeliness. Indeed, for many it has become easier to watch television on the Internet than on an actual television. Today, nearly everyone e-mails. Many people are now using Kindle to read books and periodicals—a change, a phenomenal change, from the way things used to be.

Defenders of traditional, print-based old media criticize the Internet for what they see as its shallow, unedited, anything goes, copycat coverage of events. But they also acknowledge that the Web has opened the door to unprecedented public participation in nearly every area of life while providing an audience reach far beyond the capabilities of most of the analog world.

This handbook will let you know what I have told many about how the tools and techniques of the Internet combined with conventional understanding of communications have made a major difference in lives and careers. It will also tell you how you can master this new world.

One more thing: There is no denying that those who seemed to have an intuitive grasp of this new medium and have invested in picking up operational know-how on the Web are prospering even in these uncertain economic times. Like John F. Kennedy, Bill Paley, Ronald Reagan, and Procter & Gamble, all of whom understood the new medium of TV and how it differed from radio, Barack Obama recognized the power of the Internet to reach vast numbers of voters and raise money in unprecedented amounts. It's a whole new world.

Back in the mid-1990s, the Internet represented a potential more than a mainstream tool for influence. Incidentally, by "influence," I mean the ability to attract the attention of those whose attention we need to get things done—or undone. In his 2009 book *Growing Up Digital*, Internet visionary Don Tapscott notes that back around 1996, it was a totally different world, digitally speaking. There was no Google, no Facebook, no Twitter, and no BlackBerry. YouTube didn't exist; you had to watch a music video on TV. Now, there is all that and more, with new applications coming online all the time.

Yet, at the same time, traditional forms of media endure. Even in this Internet era, there are still televisions, telephones, magazines, newspapers, trade publications, in-person forums for speeches, direct mail, sales calls, flyers on our cars, and point-of-purchase displays.

The challenge is to integrate those old-style types of media with digital technology in ways that enable them to reinforce each other. This is not easy. Digital marketing expert Akin Arikan makes clear in *Multichannel Marketing* that while effectiveness from off-line strategies comes from leveraging proven formulas, in online efforts, success often comes only from trial and error. These two quite different approaches must be brought together, and that has been the convergence nut to crack in the twenty-first century.

For this handbook I decided to examine both old and new media and address the key influence issues as they pertain to five distinct groups. They are:

- Those business leaders who recognize the importance of the Internet but don't yet have their arms around it.
- Everyone in communities across the United States—from Asheville, North Carolina, to Sacramento, California, and around the world from Paris to Tokyo—who needs to view the Internet as a vehicle for career transition and personal branding.
- The digital-savvy Millennials (born between 1980 and 2001) who know technology quite well, but not how to apply it to business and organizational problems. Many of them come to my office seeking jobs, but for all of their tech savvy, too few have derived any truly marketable skills. They often cannot, or will not, connect the dots between social media and rolling out a new product for a corporation or managing a crisis. Perhaps their conception of technology is too narrow, having used it mainly for connecting with friends and entertainment.
- Those early adopters who require the fundamentals of the influence industry bundled with the tools that are available and coming online. Running Facebook or HuffingtonPost.com is very different from creating and executing a public relations or marketing campaign.
- Public relations professionals who want to rethink how they do their jobs. They may be in-house at corporations, professional-services firms, government, or nonprofits. They might work at public relations agencies. Their budgets might have been reduced and they may be being forced to produce results cheaper as well as better and in real time. Digital fits the bill.

To prepare for this, I conducted hundreds of interviews with business leaders, consumers, media heads, government officials, and college students. I buttonholed the best and brightest at the World Economic Forum (which I have attended since 1986), at the Ambrosetti Conference, and at a dozen more major events, looking for insight on how the digital world works now and what keeps it running in that way. I research trends and issue comprehensive trend reports on a regular basis.

In addition, since 1996, I have also published full-length books on phenomena such as what's changed in power and influence, demographics, and career success, and how society identifies its heroes. Many knowledgeable people have opened their minds and hearts and let me in.

From those conversations and research, I compiled a list of what I believe are the issues most critical and useful to public relations professionals today. These are:

- The human voice required for the Internet versus the statesmanlike formal one that has been standard in professional discourse
- The demand for just-in-time content that is provocative
- How to successfully pull together all the tools available
- Linking what you want to say to the affairs of the day—in other words, to a bigger issue
- Persuading clients to adopt new approaches to gain control over their message
- Having the guts to take risks, to the point of creative destruction or blowing up what is

More specifically, I have woven all of the following concerns into the chapters of this book:

- *The need for a transition from business as a controlled, tightly scripted message delivered top-down to business as a conversation.* The best description of this probably is by Rick Levine, Christopher Locke, Doc Searls, and David Weinberger, authors of *The Cluetrain Manifesto.* They declared, "Markets are conversations." "Markets" refers to every space in which we advance our points of view, products, services, brands, causes, careers, and leaders. To participate in a conversation demands, well, a conversational tone—or a human voice. That requires finding our voice, as organizations, brands, and individuals, and having it resonate. It involves understanding.

- *The ability to view the universe of what we do in terms of hyperlinks.* Influence on the Web comes through the wisdom of crowds or how many others decide our content is worth linking to. This mind-set requires a shift from a competitive stance to a cooperative one. Influence is no longer a zero-sum game. It used to be that if *Newsweek* had a home-run edition, *Time* looked bad. Now if HuffingtonPost.com has a home-run post, we can all look good—i.e., have influence—by linking to it.
- *Recognizing that our audience determines what particular tools we use and how we use them.* A question such as: Is microblogging hotter than traditional blogging? is irrelevant in the public relations trenches. All that matters is what tools best help carry your message to that audience. Again, discovering just what those tools are means trial and error. In fact, in some digital circles, failure is a required rite of passage.
- *Knowing 24/7 what is being said about your company, products, services, industry, competition, and leadership on the Web.* This is a necessary investment of money and management attention. Skip a day and pay.
- *Fully understanding that lemons can be transformed into lemonade.* Attacks, misinformation, and ridicule can be opportunities to present our own takes. If Johnson & Johnson had had a deeper understanding of the Web, it might have been the winner in Motringate. Knowing how to respond includes running out what-if scenarios beforehand and creating tentative crisis communications plans. This might include having third-party allies assembled in the wings, digital sites already operating, and experienced pros ready to parachute in for tone and content.
- *Realizing that measurement depends on goals.* Clients may want to know only the number of page views, but who is being reached could be more relevant to the client's goal.

More challenging is attempting to assess how online and off-line communications are reinforcing each other. This introduces the budget. How much do we allocate to what tools, and what kinds of specialists do we hire? How do we decide on digital demographics or do they really matter in an age when eight-year-olds can use computer programs while many adults cannot?

- *Broadening the menu of genres.* Instead of using just explanatory prose, there's tremendous payoff in adopting irony, humor, parody, poetry, creative nonfiction, and more. Communication as entertainment is not one of the deadly sins. The Internet is so vast, it seems digital communications almost necessitate these new adoptions.
- *Becoming aware that course correction is the new modus operandi.* Changing a strategy or tactic is not an admission of error. It's smart. And it's necessary. Clients should demand documentation of those changes. That's evidence that the public relations professionals are paying attention.

That's just a broad overview. In the chapters that follow I will drill down to the nuts and bolts. Those of us who become most comfortable and nimble in cyberspace will be the influence winners. Those who hang back, stuck in an analog world, will find themselves finished, over, yesterday, without a voice.

The Internet being the evolving entity it is, I will keep bringing readers up-to-date on my own digital sites, including www.dilenschneiderpower.com. In addition, this book's appendix contains some suggested tactics and resources to stretch our mind-sets and enhance our skills still further. I also include a list of noteworthy resources at the end of the book.

As you read this book, select the passages that apply to you and what you want to do. Try blending your newfound knowledge with your personal creativity and you will find new and exciting ways to get your ideas across. It will be a challenge at first, but don't give up, because once you have a handle on the new forms of technology, you will prosper and benefit and have fun and, equally significant, raise your thinking to a new level.

SECTION ONE

PREREQUISITES FOR DIGITAL COMMUNICATIONS

Public relations—or the art of influence—may be as old as the human race. As our species lumbered around on two legs, the earliest humans had to get the hang of persuading others in the group to do what was necessary for survival. Those groups that were led by the more astute influencers went on to pass along their genes.

Fortunately, the art of public relations, as we know it now, has been practiced long enough for a body of knowledge and wisdom to be collected. Today, anyone who wants to have influence can obtain information about the discipline; observe how it operates in fields ranging from business to the arts; and experiment with basic strategies and tactics. The incentive to do just that frequently comes as a result of a crisis.

Back in the 1980s, mothers who lost their children to drunk drivers formed the effective, game-changing organization known as MADD. Being drunk is no longer a joke. When it happens behind the wheel, it's illegal. More recently, the unemployed, the aged, the swindled, and youth who can't afford an education, along with their advocates, have begun orchestrating and using the media to advance a twenty-first-century populist movement. Today, public relations has become the essential tool for almost every aspect of life that requires public exposure: politics, business, culture, law, art, science, philanthropy, education—you name it.

PR has become as integral an institution to society as government, commerce, and medicine. And if planet Earth is to make it to the twenty-second century, the common good, as opposed to raw individualism, has to be served. Part of that common good is creating wealth in sustainable ways. In this current global marketplace driven by technology, no one seems to have the answers to "how" to sustain wealth creation, but public relations can open up the conversation on making, distributing, and growing economic value from our best minds—and hearts.

Good news for the common good comes from the technology front. Those with a message—personal, political, or commercial—currently have access to digital tools that are no-cost or low-cost, high-reach, and fun to use. It is even possible to be a movement of one.

Traditional media are, quite simply, under siege. Web 2.0 has produced a historic paradigm shift in how we communicate, collaborate, dispute, and engage with one another. Ideas, opinions, facts, and attention are no longer the proprietary assets of a small group of the all-powerful. Hewlett-Packard is already democratizing print publishing via its MagCloud service, which now allows anyone connected to the Internet to publish, print, promote, sell, and deliver a professional-quality magazine—on demand.

Digital applications can be used in isolation or as stand-alones. Many of the 250 million global members of Facebook have established their own universe of influence within that application. Some of them will never want, or need, to exit that networking paradise in order to advocate a cause, transmit information, connect to others, develop personal branding, cooperate on projects, raise funds, or promote an enterprise. On Christmas Eve 2008, Facebook had a record amount of traffic—an indication that the virtual space may have provided a greater sense of security and comfort than the real space of holiday events. On the other hand, there are those who will find it useful to combine digital tools with the more traditional ones associated with public relations.

If effectiveness from this convergence of new media with old media came merely from following directions, then everyone who wanted influence would have it—in spades. That isn't the case, of course. The practice of public relations is filled with those who aren't being heard or won't be.

This book helps anyone who wants influence to develop the mind-set, intuitive grasp, confidence, strategies, and tactics to bring together all available and emerging tools. Those who get the hang of it will not only survive, but contribute to the common good, as well as their own good. Those who do not will find themselves voiceless and ignored—individually and as groups. Influence is power. Lack of it is powerlessness.

The nineteen chapters of this handbook are divided into four sections. Section 1 introduces the basics, or the nuts and bolts, of digital technology, ranging from how to monitor the Web to operating blogs and microblogs (tweets).

CHAPTER

WEBSITES

"Know your message, audience/customer, and yourself *before* configuring digital sites and creating content."

—JONATHAN ZIMMERMAN

IT SEEMS COUNTERINTUITIVE: The least critical factor in digital communications success is the technology. But that's the reality. The technology has been around since 1996, when the Internet began emerging as a commercial messaging and marketing tool.

Overall, the winners in digital communications have *not* been those with the best technology, the best IT consultants, and the most money invested in getting and keeping the technical edge. Those hitting the home runs have been the strategic plodders who took the time to try out different personas, simplification techniques, keywords, attention-grabbing tactics, rhythms, and timing. Those who succeed are those who keep at it and those who take the offense and not just play defense. They range from site aggregator Matt Drudge to political blogger Markos Moulitsas. They understand that the Web presents a unique opportunity to make a human connection.

Jonathan Zimmerman provides The Dilenschneider Group's clients a unique perspective on today's changing modes of communication across diverse global business environments. He uses his expertise in current and emerging online communications technologies to explain over and over again that winning strategies flow from certain key basics. Those clients must:

- *Know who they are.* Digital sites are all about putting a human face on leadership, companies, brand names, causes, products, services, and fund-raising campaigns. The face will only come across as fully human if the site owners or authors let it. Never has the dictum "Know thyself" been more critical.
- *Know what the message is.* Every aspect of the website, from design to word choice to interactive capability, should serve to communicate a central message. That message might be "We're a fun group," "We're here for Mom and Dad," or "Company X gets results." A site launched before a message is clarified and

agreed upon will end up sending too many messages, with none catching on. Those mixed signals can only confuse, distract, and ultimately, undermine credibility.

- *Know who the audience/customer is.* This is tricky. Clients might assume they have a particular constituency or target market down cold. But it isn't until the effort fails that they recognize that many ostensibly homogeneous groups often contain considerable diversity. That might be subtle, but it counts—a lot. Booz & Company consultants Richard Rawlinson and Natasha Kuznetsova have written that the over-50 market isn't a monolith. As they explain in their 2009 *Strategy + Business* article "50 Plus: A Market That Marketers Still Miss," the attitudes of people age 50 and older have been shaped by that specific generation's formative experiences. This is why testing out or launching a beta version/mini-site (a single web page that is small, contained, and very specific) to see if your new product, brand, or service resonates amongst members of your target audience is a "must do."

Zimmerman coaches organizations to approach websites as the complex strategic projects they are. The goal of a site might be to promote awareness of addictive behavior; to sell more public relations services or condos; to raise funds for scholarships; or to create a community for stay-at-home mothers. But that goal can only be achieved through the human touch. For organizations that have operated as "all business," finding their humanity, as the Web demands, will take work.

The appropriate technical choices will flow from that work. Usually, the technology doesn't have to be state-of-the-art or even expensive. Incidentally, that's a lesson that Big High-Tech has been learning: Consumers understand that "gee whiz" and pricey have little to do with the success of digital outreach. That's exactly why the netbook has captured a growing share of the laptop market. It's got just enough technology to get the job done.

This chapter presents guidelines for websites and processes that create the "we-and-you" bond. The primary focus will be on the formal website. That website used to be a static entity with information about the organization or the product or service. Now, as competition increases and knowledge about digital communications catches on, websites are evolving into an almost "anything goes" modality.

WEB PRESENCE

As readers probably already realize, a website is not only about transmitting information, advocating a cause, or selling a product/service. It's about communicating a presence or the compelling message about what the organization represents. What follows are some steps that help create the right presence.

STEP 1: PLANNING

Planning entails:

- *Having a deep understanding of all the intangibles, ranging from who the organization is to who the audience/customer is.* That level of understanding could require experiential research, or it could flow automatically from the organization and its leadership. Mediabistro.com, which serves the freelance writing community, knew who its audience was and who looked to it for help. Founder Laurel Touby, once herself a struggling freelancer, sold the site to Jupitermedia (now renamed WebMediaBrands) for about $23 million in 2007, at a time when many other digital entrepreneurs were still struggling with the monetizing issue.
- *Analyzing other successful websites, including the competition's.* Discern what factors make for success, and imitate the best practices. Checking out what's out there that's working should be done on a regular basis.
- *Deciding what approach or approaches will reach the right audiences in the most efficient and effective way.* That might be accomplished by providing a great deal of relevant

information or perspectives about an issue. It might be through giving visitors to your site access to links where they can find their own information. It might be through conversations or enabling user-created content. It might be through providing an entertaining experience. Or it might be a combination of all of these techniques.

STEP 2: CONTENT

When making decisions about content, organizations should strive to communicate conversationally and through very simple concepts and language. The disembodied corporate voice and ossified brand identity are out of touch with trends toward more customer interaction and participation. Keep this advice in mind:

- The look and the text of a website should not be that of traditional advertising or boilerplate messaging. Remember, digital "sells" through the human touch. Conventional commercial techniques will turn off customers. So will tired branding or unsubtle, hard-charging efforts to sell.
- If the organization is presented as a "we," then the audience/customer must be addressed as a "you." Actually, the "we" and "you" is the preferred approach since the objective is to engage customers in a personalized experience, seemingly custom-made for them.
- Content should enlighten through seduction, not preach or overwhelm with expertise. That means keeping text simple and avoiding professional jargon. The objective is not to impress with an insider's knowledge of language and concepts. That only creates a top-down or smartest-guy-in-the-room tone. Rather, the objective is having the reader feel comfortable and at home with your business—a peer, as it were. Select the best, and only the best, support material to make a point. Don't overargue your case to your audience. Less is more.
- Techniques of oral communications or speechwriting/scriptwriting can be highly effective. That means using contractions, sentence fragments, short statements, and

breaking up text with devices such as rhetorical questions, wit, and brief anecdotes. Your website should strive to capture the tone of one human being talking face-to-face with another.

STEP 3: GRAPHICS

When selecting images or graphics, again, less is more.

- Use only as many images or graphics as are necessary to support, reinforce, or highlight text, as well as make the web page attractive. Don't visually bombard your site visitors.
- Good pictures can speak a thousand words. If a photo or other image will save a lot of explaining, then use it instead of text. Remember, our society is moving in the direction of post-word communication, and words and their meanings are being continually reconfigured by the net-generation (also known as Millennials and digital natives) through text messaging.
- If the objective is to just throw candid snapshots out there, then that's fine. The site can appear very casual and haphazardly thrown together. Otherwise, avoid appearing amateurish.

STEP 4: DESIGN

The design of the website should not exist as an end in itself, but as a tool to create a presence and a total impression. In fact, a design that is too prominent can distract and actually annoy site visitors. In making design decisions:

- Never make the audience/customer exert effort or have "to work" to get whatever it is they want or need from the site. That's the overriding principle here.
- Avoid clutter or wearing out the reader. That can be done through use of white or negative space. In *Layers Magazine*'s "Negative Space," graphic designer Jacob Cass writes: "Whether it's a logo, a magazine page, or a website, sometimes

the things you don't design are more powerful than the things you do. This is often achieved by the use of negative space." Negative space is, in itself, a design element.

- Never use dark text on dark backgrounds or, for that matter, colored text on a white background. Black-on-white makes for the easiest read.
- Increase readability by making text concise, breaking up dense text, and making sure text is laid out in a simple manner.
- Choose colors carefully, since color can overwhelm as well as distract.
- Use color profiling, or colors that depict your industry or the message you are trying to deliver.
- If audio and video can assist the audience, use them. But make sure they are easy for readers to access. Material that loads slowly or that is of poor quality will drive visitors away from your site.

Navigation

There are other important design elements related to getting around a website. Making navigation of a site easy and even fun will attract more visitors, keep them on your site longer during each visit, move them to return, and, through word-of-mouth and word-of-mouse, encourage others to stop by.

- *Menus.* Every web user is familiar with menus and how they work. They are usually found on the left side of web pages in vertical format. They may include clickable buttons linked to products or categories, blog pages, glossaries, size charts, or shipping tables—anything that appears on the site's other web pages. A site map can be provided and is recommended for large sites, but it must retain the personality of the rest of the site. The objective is to have a seamless "look and feel" across all pages.
- *Tabs.* A horizontal row of file folders, or tabs, should be placed at the top of web pages to give users easy access to popular content. This format is almost essential for massive sites.

- *Two-Click Rule.* It shouldn't require more than two clicks for visitors to reach any page on the site. Every page of the site should be at most only two clicks away from the home page.

The Launch

When the Internet was new, it was almost imperative to register with major search engines. Nowadays, site designers can get the "Google juice" flowing intuitively by selecting a domain name or URL that specifically relates to what the site is about and by being savvy about tone, rhythm, content, and keywords.

1. *Use search engine optimization to improve search results.* Sites have to be optimized for the search engine spiders and crawlers to notice them and pick them up. Optimization means:
   - Incorporating keywords in the text material on every page, as well as topical references and names of popular subjects. That increases the odds that search engines will pick up the content.
   - Having each web page contain the keywords and phrases that your customers are most likely going to key into search engines when they want to find information, perspectives, or providers of products and services. Here, you have to enter the mind of the audience/customer. As the operator of the site, you might be thinking "public relations services," but your audience/customers might be thinking "promoting your business," "creating brand identity," "personal branding," or "public relations on the cheap." The wrong keywords could prevent a site from receiving any traffic.
   - Making sure the individual keywords and phrases are in the meta-tag description of the site. This is built into the code along with the design or site-builder software.
   - Avoiding overcrowding of your keyword list.
2. *Don't use "home page" in the title.* That decreases search engine rankings. The objective is to be listed on the first two pages of a search engine, ideally among the first ten items.

The higher the ranking, the better. Most people assume that if an organization consistently receives top spots on search engines, then the company must be doing something right. That assumption can turn casual online browsers into buyers.

PROMOTING THE SITE

New sites are like new stores. Whether your presence is in cyberspace or in a physical space, you have to let people know that you are there. This takes time, so plan ahead to have your website up and running before it is needed as a key part of a promotional plan. Some tips and ideas:

- Use all promotional tactics, including postcards, e-mail blasts, cold calls, freebies, discounts, contests, links to any related blogs, cobranding, mainstream media articles, interviews, commentary, hard news, and your own press releases. Also, notify other sites—particularly those communities dealing with your subject—and ask them to link to your site. Then keep doing what's working.
- Use Twitter.com to announce the new site and highlight its content.
- Leverage membership in social networks and special-interest online communities to bring traffic to your site. If your organization is not currently a member, become one in several networks. A useful guide is *The Truth About Profiting from Social Networking*, by Patrice-Anne Rutledge. One company that has profitably harnessed the promotional power of social networking is Procter & Gamble. P&G is behind a large online community of teenage girls called Beinggirl.com ("For Girls, By Girls") where the consumer giant's major line of feminine-care products is effectively spotlighted. The popular site features an "Ask Iris" advice column, music downloads (through a partnership with Sony), online games, and discussion zones called "Girl Talk." Hewlett-Packard is another major company in the vanguard of this movement. It currently hosts scores of online forums for a global army of customers.

In an average month, these forums have attracted as many as 5 million page views, more than 10,000 posts from customers, and some 400,000 searches.

- Deal with controversial subjects. On the Web especially, with its many hyperlinks and viral nature, this seems to be a uniquely effective technique in getting attention.
- Post provocative content with the right keywords, topical references, and brand names—often and throughout the day. Using a content management system, instead of HTML code, makes this approach more feasible.
- Design sections for reader input that encourage interactivity. This is a way to increase the odds that the site will be noticed, talked about, and visited. First, however, decide if that user input can be posted as anonymous and if it will be screened before being made public.

MONITORING THE SITE

Unless the organization intends to sell advertising on the website, exact measures of traffic and who's visiting aren't necessary. A rudimentary service will usually be adequate to track traffic. There are paid services and free ones, such as Google Analytics.

What's more important is to monitor traffic often, throughout the day, and to focus more on what is pulling in visitors and less on what is being ignored. Analyzing the traffic a site gets, and what attracts it, can provide a gold mine of insight into a product or subject, a profession, an industry, and even the competition.

If the site is being used to build a database of names or information about visitors, then it is important to have a mechanism that captures this data in a form that is useful. Many site operators launch sites just to generate such databases. That information is frequently so valuable to marketers that it can be sold, but only with the visitors' permission.

TAKEAWAYS

- Digital communications succeed or fail based on the self-knowledge of the author, deep understanding of the audience/market, and creating the right message.
- Websites are an organization's human face to the world. (Emphasis is on human.)
- Mini-experiments usually are necessary before a major launch of a website.
- Less is more. That applies to every aspect of a site, from language to graphics.
- Investing time and effort in planning, launching, promoting, tracking, and continually fine-tuning or overhauling your site can have a huge payoff.

CHAPTER

BLOGS AND MICROBLOGS

"Blogs and more recently microblogs have made the influence playing field flat. Anyone who understands how to write for a digital medium, has the courage to deal with provocative topics with a unique voice, and is passionate about posting often can be heard—and has been changing the balance of power in the world of business, politics, religion, academia, and more."

—Art Gormley

BLOGS AND MICROBLOGS like Twitter have changed the sphere and scope of influence and power more than any other popular digital application, including Facebook. By putting the tools of influence and power in the hands of everyman and everywoman, these applications have changed everything in public relations, public affairs, marketing communications, and actual selling. To succeed you have to learn and be part of this world.

The democratic quality of the Internet, and the resulting flattening of the influence playing field, as described by digitally savvy Art Gormley, a longtime colleague at The Dilenschneider Group, means that money or capital, contacts, family pedigree, Ivy League education, and a senior title at a public relations agency, lobbying firm, or marketing communications boutique have become, to some extent, irrelevant.

Worldly education is as important today as formal education.

What is keeping the so-called "professionals" and "experts" in digital communications in demand, as well as providing digital entrepreneurial opportunities for visionaries, is their experience in creating the message, positioning that message "just right" for diverse constituencies, testing all that out, selecting what might be most effective and cost-efficient for the right target audience using the right tools—and then being able to jump in with immediate course correction, as necessary.

The message is still king. But now it must increasingly be shaped for a digital medium. For too many older professionals in the PR field, it has not been an easy transition. Like the early radio programmers and actors who approached the new medium of television by statically reading scripts, too many of today's PR experts are superimposing the proven ways of analog on a digital world. For that reason, clients are not always getting the results they should.

This chapter explores how blogs and microblogs can be used in messaging. It will also discuss how these two technologies can be leveraged to reinforce each other, as well as complement what's known as "old media."

BLOGS AND TWITTER

In mid-March 2009, the editors of TechCrunch.com, a hugely popular blog site, estimated that there were 133 million blogs in existence. But fewer than that are being actively updated and read because they require plenty of sweat equity, along with an understanding of this medium. In addition, TechCrunch has a hunch that blogging is being made less popular by the fast-growing platform provided by Twitter. Tweeting can transmit information and perspective. It also provides the capability of a network. Those using it feel a sense of ownership, that it is their medium.

Briefly, a tweet (or microblog) is simply a short text message (of no more than 140 characters) that can be sent instantly and simultaneously, and without specific addressing (unlike an e-mail), to the cell phones and computers of a large number of recipients or so-called "followers."

Tweets can be picked up by search engines just like blogs, and through a shorthand form of URL, search engines can link tweets directly to blogs. One of Twitter's most attractive features is the challenge and fun of being able to position and package a tweet in 140 characters. A number of early blogging evangelists are now devoting more energy to tweeting than to blogging. Tweets can be monitored through BackType. A tweet's influence can be measured by Twinfluence, a tool that collects information on Twitter followers.

But, at the end of the day, the blog—or what might be likened to long-form journalism when compared to a tweet—remains the communications vehicle for most of the typical messages leaders want to put out there these days. Blogging is not going away. It will continue to evolve even while facing competition for eyeballs, as well as minds and hearts, from newer messaging platforms.

A growing number of movers and shakers, such as economist Nouriel Roubini—also known as Dr. Doom—use both blog posts and Twitter to get out their message. In a March 2009 *Portfolio Magazine* article titled "The Prime of Mr. Nouriel Roubini," writer Helaine Olen cites Roubini as an economist who knows how to go about the "business of publicity."

WHAT IS A BLOG?

There are, in fact, numerous reasons to explain the rapid growth and acceptance of blogs, which Paul Chaney and Richard Nacht discuss in their book *Realty Blogging: Build Your Brand and Outsmart Your Competition.* Many business sectors such as residential real estate, which relies to a considerable extent on the human touch and word-of-mouth and advertising, now do use blogs to reach their respective audiences. Considering its many advantages, it is not at all difficult to understand why blogging has taken off so quickly and effectively. In the end, a little hard work, dedication, and persistence can ultimately pay off handsomely for the commercial blogger.

First, and perhaps most significantly, blogging is very inexpensive compared to traditional media. It can cost as little as $5 monthly and sometimes nothing at all. Moreover, because the fast-growing medium has already gained so much traction, it is often unnecessary to shell out any payments to be recognized by the major search engines such as Google and Bing.

Equally important from a technological perspective, blogging is relatively easy. Digital Immigrants and even technophobes can readily launch, maintain, and update a blog. Although most websites have until now used HTML (hypertext markup language), which requires some training and has a learning curve for proficiency, an increasing number are migrating from HTML to straightforward content management systems, which allow nontechnical users to publish content.

Blogging also emphasizes the personal. It puts a human face on a product, a pitch, a personality, a cause, a service, or a brand. In short, it's much like one human being communicating directly with another. If visitors to a particular blog relate to its tone and message, the chance is high they will become buyers, volunteers, supporters, or even members of a larger blogging community.

In addition, blogging is interactive. Visitors to a blog can express their views. Operators of sites know they have scored big when visitors begin talking with each other.

According to Chaney and Nacht,

> Search engines *love* blogs. . . . Blogs, by their design, meet the current requirements for search engines and search traffic. Research shows that blogs get crawled more quickly and more often than other forms of digital content. That can be increased by posting often throughout the day, using catchy, topical headlines in the subject title, and by finding out what keywords the search engines are picking up that day. There are search engines such as Technorati solely dedicated to blogs.
>
> Blogs are niche vehicles, so they are perfect for competitive differentiation in a marketplace that has fragmented into niches (better to sell women's socks online and offline than to try to sell all types of women's clothing). Given the low cost, a blog can be created for every niche. That means several brands can be launched and maintained without confusing customers.

Blogging can be a key business development tool depending on such factors as the specific sector and size of a firm. "Blogs attract links," say Chaney and Nacht. "That increases search engine interest, reflecting the wisdom of the crowds." Commercial blogs have global reach, providing relatively easy access to non–U.S. markets. Entrepreneurs wanting to test their products or services abroad can do so at minimal cost.

HOW TO HIT HOME RUNS

Rather than having to make an either-or choice between blogging and tweeting, users should recognize that the two were never mutually exclusive. Likewise, new and old media were not intended to compete with one another in a strategic plan. Both have their place. The reality is that successful bloggers and successful tweeters use both types of messages to extend reach, including driving traffic to both platforms. In addition, those with successful public relations campaigns don't differentiate between new and old media. Promotion should be seamless. When it isn't, that's a red flag.

Instead of being sucked into competitive arguments about which vehicle has the most reach, it is best (for achieving influence) to use all the platforms available. Use more of what produces the best results—whether it is increasing sales of your services or donations to a cause.

Here are proven guidelines for getting results, quickly and at a low cost, using digital media:

- Move from a safe mind-set to one that entertains provocative and contrarian thinking. Boilerplate drives away traffic. Readers are searching for information and insight they can't obtain elsewhere—at least not easily or cheaply. If you can't make this leap from "Shut-Down Organization Man" to "Openly Creating Value Person," you shouldn't blog.
- Make the message simple and attention grabbing. In 2007, Chip and Dan Heath published a manifesto, *Made to Stick*, about how anyone or any organization can create messages that get and keep attention. So, for example, instead of writing a long-winded statement about why the organization may be laying off workers, compress it into a phrase or two that communicates the organization's values, its possible future, and its ability to start up a conversation. The Web is about two-way conversations, not isolated statements. A leak about a pending reduction in force may end up on a website like AboveTheLaw.com, where such statements can shut down any possibility of a conversation.
- Be prepared for push-back. That's part of the territory. That entails having a crisis communications plan ready for managing rumors, which is explored in greater detail throughout chapter 9.
- Be affable and genial. That's the new way to make friends as well as allies. It might help to reread Dale Carnegie's 1936 classic *How to Win Friends and Influence People.* Arrogance is outmoded. It also has no place on the Web. An ironic tone

has appeal in this era when no one knows really what will happen tomorrow and what happened yesterday may offer little or no insight about what will come down the road in the future.

- Monitor news in order to have topical headlines and links. Everything is *now.* The cycle of what's hot speeds up daily.
- Be helpful. That might mean providing direct contacts for someone out of work or detailing how-to's on submitting effective cover letters. Blogging is essentially a service medium.
- Know there is a fine line between entertainment and fact-based content.

THE MESSAGE

Messages no longer can come from the mind of the highest-ranking officer. Accept the compelling logic of the wisdom of crowds. When blogging and microblogging, messages must be created that drill down to what's in the minds and hearts of diverse constituencies. After the basic message is put together, different versions can be tested in a variety of media, both new and old. For example, consider this message: "Veterans receive free tuition at College X." Through testing, along with the comments it generated, this message morphed into "Feeding soldiers' minds—it's on us." The message is still on the drawing board as we write.

When shaping and distributing a message using blogs or Twitter, here are some additional tips:

- *Look for what resonates.* If the message you've crafted resonates among the group of brainstormers and in early testing, it could resonate among diverse groups.
- *Make it heavy on emotion.* Human beings are not, by and large, rational.
- *Target the message at the "other," not oneself.* Too many messages are self-centric.

- *Focus on solutions, not problems.* Invite input about those solutions.
- *Treat the message as a work-in-progress.* That means no cast-in-concrete rollout or distribution plan. Use more of what is working. New media are opportunistic, not formulaic.
- *Hire digital natives as interns, full-time employees, or part-timers.* Millennials will excel in tactics, because digital media is the only thing they know, but they will require training in strategic planning and client interaction.
- *Be flexible in measuring results.* There is no one best way to measure results. The objective for the early stages of a campaign might be simply to get the message out. Later in the campaign you may count the amount of donations raised, and from what geographical areas. Staying with twentieth-century ways of assessing success can be misleading and plunge the campaign into failure. The trick is educating clients about what matters, and when and how to do the counting. To discover what new approaches in measurement are available, and what they regard as significant, it's useful to interview several vendors.

* * *

Blogging and microblogging aren't for everyone. If your organization isn't suited for this transparent medium, focus on other means of shaping and distributing a message. Inept blogging and tweeting could well throw open the door to undermining the brand name.

TAKEAWAYS

- Blogs and Twitter have leveled the playing field in influence. But digital professionals are still needed to help shape, test, and monitor the distribution of the message.
- Blogs are ideally structured for putting a human face on

an enterprise; differentiating it; and implementing low-cost, high-reach promotion of anything, be it a cause, product, or service.

- Blogging and microblogging can reinforce each other. So can new and old media. All should be put to work in a campaign seamlessly.
- The message is king. Take the time to create the right message and to test it out. Get input through other digital sites.
- Blogging and tweeting aren't for everyone. Clients and prospects who aren't good candidates for this approach should not be pushed to accept it. Experience shows that investing too much energy into converting the resistant violates the 80/20 rule; that is, the lion's share of revenues comes from 20 percent of clients.

CHAPTER

MONITORING THE INTERNET

> "No matter how large an organization is, how many resources it deploys, it's impossible to monitor everything on the Internet. And it's not necessary or useful to do so."
>
> —Jonathan Zimmerman

WE LIVE IN A TECHNOLOGY-CONNECTED world that thrives on real-time information. But business leaders as well as other institutional heads must ask themselves one basic question: To what extent, if at all, do we trust the Internet?

If the answer is "not much," then the odds are that these generals of commerce are not tapping into the full advantages of this unique medium. Additionally, they are likely to be opening themselves, and the organizations they lead, to attacks from critics, customers, media, competitors, stock market manipulators, and perhaps even their own employees. Fear can propel leaders and their organizations into a downward trajectory, especially in challenging business environments. On the other hand, confidence—feeling secure and at home in the online world—is required to spot and exploit opportunities and prevent and manage potential threats.

This chapter explains why digital confidence matters and how to embed it into any organization. It presents guidance on how to monitor what's being said about, and by, a leader, company, industry, customer, prospect, competitor, supply chain partner, regulator, investor, and the macroeconomy at large.

Here is a basic approach that few practice: Tell your story, every day, over and over. Initiate. Do not just monitor and respond. Get out there. Control your environment and the dialogue about you and your company.

TRUSTING THE MEDIUM

According to the research by management consulting firm Booz & Company, the largest obstacle to businesses using the Internet is confidence. In their spring 2009 article "Watching over the Web" in

Strategy + Business, Booz consultants Thomas Künstner, Manuel Kohnstamm, and Stephan Luiten write that the single biggest factor in unleashing the Internet's potential is "not technology. It is confidence. Digital confidence is the level of trust that consumers place in this emerging infrastructure."

Successful people, in the years ahead, will be those who not just master and understand the Internet, but also use it over and over to get their point of view across.

Relying on once-successful media strategies and tactics—only doing a better job of that—brings a sense of safety and predictability. Business executives may brainstorm in conference rooms about buying ads on the Super Bowl broadcast, placing an opinion-editorial in the *Wall Street Journal*, or having their leadership interviewed by Maria Bartiromo or Chris Matthews. But what about buying ad space on Facebook or using real-time advertising? No one in the loop has to be educated about why that makes sense and could produce beneficial results for the organization and the individuals involved. There's no learning curve. The experience is innate. But it's not all that likely that boardrooms are brainstorming about anything beyond online advertising, or discussing how to encourage user-generated content, nurture online communities across and within their target markets, and allow office time for employees to blog or tweet.

In addition to not being routine, these expanded digital approaches require experimentation. No pricey report from some research firm will spell out what online strategies and tactics work and which don't. Internet marketing expert Akin Arikan explains in his book *Multichannel Marketing* that online communications require trial-and-error. Most old media strategies are proven. They may be yielding diminishing returns, but they are proven methods. On the other hand, professionals with reputations to protect, especially in these brutally competitive times, might feel foolish trying out things on the Internet. Yet that's exactly what it takes. That is what it took for the current online leaders such as Arianna Huffington to master the new medium. Huffington was ridiculed when she launched HuffingtonPost.com, but look at her overwhelming success today. Her news and blog site is one of the most widely read, linked to, and frequently cited destinations on the Internet.

There's more. Since this medium mutates continually, trial-and-error never ends. Mistakes are going to happen—plenty of them. But that has always been the situation in high-tech businesses. That's why players in Silicon Valley put such value on serial failure and alpha and beta versions of their products and services are a necessary rite of passage. The assumption is: If you're failing, you're learning. Actually, learning is the currency not only of the Internet, but the whole new economy.

PLAYING IN THE TRAFFIC

So, how can those fearfully holding back from the Internet come to trust it? There is only one answer: Jump in—and play in the traffic. Being a willing player, who both participates in and observes online activities, trumps all the services that are available, for free or for purchase, to monitor the Internet.

Jonathan Zimmerman notes that "no matter how large an organization is and what resources it deploys, one can't monitor everything. The reality is, it's unnecessary and not helpful." Zimmerman has a background in entrepreneurship and global strategy and is an Associate with The Dilenschneider Group. He has witnessed situations in which too many employees, contract workers, and interns in an organization surfed the Web too often and still didn't pick up on what they should have.

Why is being a hands-on player so useful? Being a player on the Internet provides direct experience with the tone, content, and pace of this medium. Although leaders probably do not have the time to devote a significant portion of their schedule to this activity, they can designate team members who do. That ensures there are those within the organization who understand the Web and how it's constantly changing, and in what fresh directions it might migrate. In itself, that ensures that the organization won't be digitally tone-deaf and a victim of learning lethargy, and it may prevent attacks, or at least help prepare your organization for handling bad consequences should they happen.

When businesses are oblivious to the unique ethos of the Internet, they become chronic victims. Here are some examples:

- The president of a marketing communications boutique was invited to facilitate a conversation on a bulletin board on Mediabistro.com. The topic concerned how the members could improve their pitches for getting jobs and assignments in publishing. His tone was that he was a successful insider while everyone else was a rookie. Members went postal. Had he more online experience, he would have known that web conversations are horizontal and inclusive and about the "we"; they cannot be vertical or top-down directives, no matter who you are.
- An owner of a medium-size fashion-design firm posted banner ads attacking competitors through sarcastic humor. The tone was perceived as caustic and not really in good humor. Within two days, he took down the ads. He had not heeded the advice of his in-house team members, who knew that irony would have been welcome, but not the negativity of the humor he used.
- An MBA student used her blog to promote herself for corporate jobs. She put herself out there as the Professional Woman. It is a case of a web persona gone wrong. The parodying was so severe that she shut down the blog and is considering legally changing her name. Parody is a powerful and cruel weapon on the Internet.

The good news is that these blunders pushed those ambitious people to grow and learn. But trauma isn't required to open up to the Web's possibilities and threats. Here are some exercises that can embed new routines in the organization and boost confidence in the Internet:

- *Analyze competitors' online communications, from their official websites to webcasts and YouTube videos.* What are they doing to send a particular message to their target listeners? What tactics are effective and which appear ineffective? In his seminal 2006 book, *Guide to Integrated Communications*, Manfred Bruhn asserted that the new competition is less about one company's products and services versus another's. Instead, it has become more about how one company's communications deliver the right message about the quality, integrity, and pricing of the products and services versus another's. Every aspect of online communications sends a message. If it's not the right message for the right constituency at the right time, the organization loses.

- *Routinely identify online sites that provide information, insight, and perspective on your organization's target audiences or markets.* These sources provide access to the mind-set of people on the Web. They can also be a harbinger of a mood shift happening online and may signal a pending attack on the organization. Of course, those go-to sites may change from time to time, so constant monitoring is a necessity.

- *Designate employees to experiment with the company's and their own personal sites.* Once underutilized for communicating information about the organization, the formal corporate website has now evolved into an almost anything-goes branding tool. Content management systems as an alternative to HTML coding have made it simpler for just about anyone to input and update web content. That can geometrically expand a site's messaging capability and potential benefits in return.

- *Use an intranet or wiki site to allow employees to share their observations and lessons learned.* Of course, there will be guidelines for what kind of tone and subject matter are appropriate, according to their fit with the organizational culture. The fewer guidelines the better. One organization instructs its digital front lines, "Be wise, yet be bold."

- *Join and participate in user groups.* Since these groups are usually clearly defined niches, they can provide an unusual peek into an organization's constituency or target market. Usually identity can be maintained as anonymous.

- *Push for an invitation to be a member of a panel on Internet communications.* Industry-level participation forces a business to learn—fast.

- *Leverage the wisdom of the crowds to create ideas and value.* Throughout the organization, form a number of salons with employees, customers, suppliers, community members, and even shareholders to bat around thinking about the digital era. The group might start a site to capture its collective wisdom.
- *Put together virtual networks.* Online contacts are often more useful than in-the-flesh ones. They usually bring to the organization's attention negative items and can pitch in with positive postings if your organization comes under attack.

MONITORING TOOLS

The best monitoring practices today might be slow and inefficient tomorrow. At the time of this book's publication, here's what is known:

- The right keywords are everything. And not all are equally productive. As an example, to find out what customers are thinking about the loan industry, the keyword to plug in is "borrowing" or "consumer debt." That focuses on the activities of the consumer, not those of the organization. And that's what's of interest.
- There are standard keywords, including the names the organization is known by: for example, McDonald's as well as Mickey D's. Standard keywords also include the names of top executives, products, services, competitors and their products and services, government watchdogs, and regulatory agencies for your industry.
- There are just-in-time keywords to capture digital activity on developing situations, such as a "product recall," "profits report," and "competitive ventures."
- Keywords can be tracked automatically in a number of ways using such vehicles as Google News, Yahoo! News, MSN News, PubSub 2.0 (when operational), and Technorati. Your organization can sign up for Google and Yahoo e-mail alerts to track and report on keywords that you specify. RSS

feeds can also be custom-made to catch keywords. Commonly translated as "really simple syndication," RSS is a family of web-feed formats used to publish frequently updated works—such as blog entries, news headlines, audio, and video—in a standardized format. Yahoo! Pipes is a service for setting up a "pipeline" that collects and presents information not only from search engines, but also microblogs such as Twitter and photo-sharing sites.

- Tracking services are increasingly becoming niche-based. That's because it is now recognized and accepted that the Internet operates via niches, which tend to seep into other categories. Niche-tracking tools include Google Finance, which brings up mentions of any particular stock price movement, and Tweet Scan, which brings up posts on specific keywords such as "Pepsi Max" or using the TweetDeck search mechanism. For YouTube, you need only key in http://youtube.com/rss/tag/+[keyword].rss. For comments on blogs, which search engines often don't pick up, there's BackType. After a keyword is entered, the site returns information on what major search engines find for that keyword in terms of blogs and web pages.
- Investigate which niche message boards and forums to track by checking out ForumFind.com, Big-Boards.com, BoardTracker.com, iVillage, Yahoo! Message Boards, MSN Money, and BoardReader.com.
- Social media sites can be tracked through Serph.com, which frequently catches what major search engine alerts might not. For example, it retrieves results from Delicious and Digg.com—two social media offerings that allow users to bookmark resources that they find useful. Such systems rank resources based on their perceived utility rather than the number of external links pointing to them.
- Find out the sites—and new ones are popping up daily—that provide customer and even employee reviews of a particular business or industry. Current favorites range from Yelp to rateAPartner.

- Check Wikipedia relating to one's own company and related topics, at least daily. This site is a favorite of mischief-makers, muckrakers, and potential enemies.
- Keep current on negative feedback about competitors on BizRate, eBay, and Amazon.

* * *

At the end of the day, it's not what is being said about a company or its leader on the Internet or how soon you discover those postings. What matters is how the organization handles that information. Successfully managing an attack or criticism requires a commitment to be a player on the Internet. Once company leaders have confidence in their ability to deal with potential threats coming from the Internet, they'll also find ways to create new value and opportunities online. And this confidence will resonate throughout the organization. Other chapters in this handbook, especially chapters 9 and 10, on rumor management and crisis communications, respectively, present additional guidelines for monitoring the Internet.

TAKEAWAYS

- Are you telling your story online?
- Confidence in the Internet as a medium determines the ability of an organization to leverage this tool to fend off attacks and otherwise obtain market advantage. This trust comes from hands-on participation in all things online. The expression "playing in the traffic" applies.
- Most errors, some costly to reputations and profits, come from businesses being digitally tone-deaf. The Web has a unique, ever-evolving ethos about how to present oneself and one's information, insight, recommendations, and cautions.
- It is impossible, and not particularly productive, to track everything that is being said about an organization and related topics online.

- Web-based monitoring tools are continually changing. Do a search on the term "Internet monitoring" or some variations of that phrase to discover new services.
- What counts is not what's said about an organization or when it is discovered, but how that information is managed. Wise handling can, by itself, build confidence.

CHAPTER

MEASUREMENT— WHY, WHAT, HOW

"Much of the current interest in measurement arises from the need to justify public relations in the organizational setting. Everyone wants to know how we add value to the business and what we accomplish. Whether it's a corporation, city hall, or the local Salvation Army, every organization wants to know what it is getting for the funds associated with public relations. These days they want to know how to do more with less, using 'smart' public relations."

—Joseph A. Kopec

IN 1988, A COMMUNICATIONS company conducted a survey of senior executives at public relations agencies and in corporate departments of public relations. An amazing 41 percent of those responding indicated that they believed that measuring the impact of public relations is "next to impossible." Today, those who want to hold on to a job or an account would never indicate, in public at least, skepticism or cynicism about why measurement is imperative, that the function can be carried out effectively and cost-efficiently, and that tracking can generate unique insights for improving results as well as ongoing performance.

ACCOUNTING FOR DOLLARS SPENT

A commitment to measurement, explains The Dilenschneider Group's senior consultant Joseph A. Kopec, "arises from the need to justify public relations in the organizational setting. Whether it's a corporation, city hall, or the local Salvation Army, whether it's the CEO or a line manager of a service organization, every organization and person wants to know what it is getting for the funds associated with public relations. These days they want to know how to do more with less, using 'smart' public relations." Usually before he actually counsels organizations and individuals, Kopec explains up front how outputs or outcomes can be measured. That in itself creates trust between the public relations adviser and clients.

Introducing the subject of metrics early in the process frequently makes clients more receptive to recommendations based on agreed-upon results. Those suggestions are usually about experimenting with new approaches, including digital strategies. More specifically, the metrics conversation can and often does deliver these messages:

- We care about your money as much as you do.
- We know what really counts in communications and how to gather and interpret the data. More than that, we can tell you what to do next to optimize your results.
- We want you to be able to justify your expenditures. Tabulation of results and how they can be interpreted are quantitative information that can be presented to management, boards of directors, shareholders, employees, members, contributors, government, and the media.

INFORMATION AVAILABLE

Not quite as clear are the underlying issues about what to measure and how. The problem is not lack of information. Kopec points out that "a tremendous reservoir of information—much of it free—is available. The Institute for Public Relations, through its Essential Knowledge Project, provides many free documents at www.instituteforpr.org."

One excellent booklet, prepared specifically for the Institute, is "Guidelines for Measuring Relationships in Public Relations," by Linda Childers Hon and James E. Grunig. Although published in 1999, it presents ideas that remain useful, such as focusing on relationships with key constituencies. Perhaps you want to measure the increase in trust with Main Street or among single women ages 18–39. That's what counts. There are almost an infinite number of ways to measure positive and negative developments in relationships, ranging from polling to driving traffic from that demographic to a website where information can be captured in a database.

A more recent article in the April 2009 edition of MIT's *Technology Review*, "But Who's Counting?" by Jason Pontin, discusses how Google and start-up Quantcast are addressing what to count and how to count it in communications on the Web. These questions range from "Does number of unique visitors matter?" to "What is the bulletproof way to compute traffic?" Depending on who was doing the counting, the online audience for *Forbes* magazine circa 2006 ranged from 6 million to 20 million per month.

Then there's the 2008 book *Multichannel Marketing: Metrics and Methods for On and Offline Success*, by Internet expert Akin Arikan. It shows the way to view and measure the synthesis of traditional and digital approaches. Arikan reminds those in the influence and marketing fields that digital outreach often has to be followed up with nondigital campaigns. And traffic on a website is meaningless if site visitors aren't converted into buyers or those who take other forms of action.

CONFIDENCE FOR MAKING JUDGMENT CALLS

The problem is having the confidence to make the judgment call about what counts, and therefore what should be measured, and about what the most productive and cost-efficient tools are for doing that. That confidence—and clients pick up on it—comes from:

- Understanding how both old and new media operate. This doesn't come from reading an article. It comes from hands-on work in the trenches. Digital natives (that is, the Millennial generation) and those who have never dealt with print journalists frequently have gaps in knowledge about the advantages of building relationships with, say, the editorial board at *BusinessWeek*. Traditional public relations strategists contend their clients only want to be interviewed by establishment editors at *Forbes*, not the flamboyant authors at Politico.com. Conversely, the Google generation can give a client dozens of ways to move products and opinions using new media techniques. They argue quite convincingly that it is faster and possibly less expensive.

- Conducting pilot projects about how old and new media can reinforce each other. Pilots are a way to gain experience with, for example, designating the platform for starting a campaign. Should it be in print and broadcast or digital? Does the tone need to be changed when a digital initiative migrates to prime-time TV talk shows?

- Continually interviewing vendors and media insiders for information about what vehicles are available, at what cost.

If buying television time is relatively low and there are good contacts with network and cable producers, this might be a core strategy in introducing a message.

- Staying current with the rapid changes in all media and how those changes impact one another. How is the exploding popularity of Twitter affecting other social networks such as Facebook and readership of print and digital trade media?
- Staying current with the younger news demographic, ages 18–25, to determine what their criticisms are.

WHAT COUNTS

In a more timid era of public relations, when professionals frequently functioned as order-takers, the question of "What counts?" usually had a simple answer: What clients perceived to be important.

Nowadays, there are digital visionaries such as Thomas Gensemer, managing partner of Blue State Digital. Best known for building the Democratic Party's online Campaign '08, Gensemer probably will go down in history for documenting that what counts is the individual voter. Influence, as Gensemer sees it, is a one-to-one message. That starts with building the database and continues with communicating through all media with this one person with appropriate pitches.

Another visionary is Chris Anderson, editor in chief of *Wired* magazine. In his 2006 book *The Long Tail—Why the Future of Business Is Selling Less of More*, Anderson says what counts is ongoing influence or sales. This is the antithesis of having a best-selling product or service as a goal, or a major media campaign aimed at an influence grand slam. Essentially, this is the gospel according to niches. What to measure, then, is what's happening (or not happening) in those niches over the longer term. This doesn't rule out the possibility of a surge to fame and fortune. It just doesn't count that as a necessary goal. Economic development expert Richard Florida addressed his early writings, such as 2002's *The Rise of the Creative Class*, to the policy makers' niche. Now, his appeal is broader.

Confident communications advisers will persuade clients on what counts and that will determine the allocation of resources. For example, in advising a midsize Connecticut law firm about developing reach to purchasers of legal services, the communications expert would specify that what counts includes:

- The reach within the state. A national reputation is irrelevant. Therefore, digital keywords, tone, content, and links will be related, shall we say, to Connecticut. Web communications are ideal for local publicity. That publicity can be reinforced with interviews in mainstream state and city media, opinion-editorials in regional publications, special events within the state, appearances on local access channels, and membership in state service and professional organizations.
- The names of those in the state likely to use various legal services (e.g., DUI defense, divorce, custody representation). Yes, investing in database information is a must.
- Contacts within all branches of state government. That entails socializing, volunteering, fund-raising, and contributing contacts. Other constituencies might also be useful, such as charitable and religious organizations.
- Word-of-mouth from satisfied clients. That means obtaining feedback from and maintaining contact with clients.

What doesn't necessarily count?

- Overall traffic to digital sites. It's not a numbers game but an influence one. Who's visiting? Who's not visiting? That must be determined.
- Relationships with constituencies not likely to bring in business. Widespread name recognition is not the goal. Having the brand known to likely purchasers and their networks is.
- Reputation for anything but results and integrity. Usually those with pressing legal matters do not shop price.
- Corporate social responsibility. Leave that to Big Law.

HOW TO COUNT

The bottom line on how to count is to measure in ways that will keep improving results and that are cost-efficient.

Sticking with the example of that midsize Connecticut law firm, in this case what needs to be counted are increasing the number of new clients, retaining current clients (particularly through cross-selling), and informational contacts from prospects. This can be done in the most rudimentary fashion; that is, simply tracking. That means that the communications expert doesn't have to recommend the law firm install exotic software to monitor visitors to digital sites. But it does mean that updating databases and collecting contact information at special events are worth the investment. Business and leads from both should be tracked, especially where they came from, in order to gain insight about the more effective tactics. Is it the website or the seminar on child custody in Stamford, Connecticut, that is bringing in the most new clients?

If the numbers go south, then the law firm must reverse engineer its strategies and tactics to identify and fix the weak spots and test out new approaches. Counting has to provide value to improve performance, not just obtain immediate results. For smaller organizations, elaborate sets of measurements aren't useful because they won't have to be presented to board members and other decision makers who have to be persuaded of anything.

Small trade associations, professional-services boutiques, or solo practitioners typically ask whether they should aim to boost traffic to their digital assets. The answer goes back to influence or marketing objective. Since they are usually niche players, large numbers per se shouldn't be the focus. Rather, the concerns should be: Are the right kinds of visitors coming? Are they taking the appropriate action, such as calling for information, joining, buying, or linking the site with related ones? And how can their numbers be increased? Here, what could be assessed are the kinds and numbers of visitors and the results of experiments for augmenting those numbers. For this, the organization can interview several vendors for a description of their services and pricing.

Kopec finds the system recommended by Gyroscope Consultancy (London) helpful for larger organizations. Gyroscope is a worldwide communications and change management firm whose clients include Coca-Cola, McDonald's Europe, and the U.K. Department for Work and Pensions. The system has three parts: tracking input, output, and outcome.

According to Gyroscope's managing director, Tom Wells:

- *Inputs* are measures of what was done to make the communications happen. They range from press releases issued to calls made to TV producers of talk shows.
- *Outputs* are measures of how many people called the 800-number to donate or how many visited the website. Where exact numbers are important, the medium used can be tracked, so you can measure outputs by designating different phone numbers, e-mail addresses, or snail-mail codes.
- *Outcomes* measure impacts. What was the change in attitude or the increase in contributions? Often this measure isn't exact. Usually it provides evidence of a correlation, not proof of a cause–effect relationship. The public service announcements about donating to the SPCA might have been related to the 15 percent boost in donations. But there were likely other causal factors, too. The appeal may have been enhanced because there were two blizzards when the ads were aired and the cold weather prompted donations for sheltering homeless animals. The death of a beloved racing horse or some other news event may have raised interest in animal causes, or perhaps an improvement in the economy simply helped donations.

Wells notes that the ratio between input and output demonstrates the efficiency of resources while the relationship between outcomes indicates the effectiveness.

Another approach to tracking does not use numbers. It is impressionistic. Entrepreneurs and artists often rely on this method to make decisions about where to put their resources, especially sweat equity. Sometimes it's called having "golden guts." A natural gift for feeling through a situation and observing can provide all the information that's needed.

Sometimes that works. Sometimes it doesn't. But everything changes. Those operating intuitively might find that the enterprise has become too large or complex to navigate without external ways to measure. At that phase of development, the enterprise should interview public relations agencies and other kinds of consultants to find out what kind of tracking systems they can provide, what their systems will help accomplish, and how much they cost.

NO ONE WAY

The collapse of so many traditional business models, in everything from financial services to law, has demonstrated that there is no single best approach, formula, or practice. At least not in this time, when there is so much global transition for most of society's institutions. That throws the burden of experimentation—which needs to be continuous—on the shoulders of both the professionals and those who use their services. You have to be in the trenches to find out what you need to know. Usually that learning process is inefficient and frustrating. That's one incentive to measure what can be measured. Having data can make decision making about means and ends less difficult and expensive. It can also enhance the credibility of the professional in the eyes of the client.

TAKEAWAYS

- In a cost-conscious global economy, in which nothing is certain, measuring has become imperative in public relations. Prospects and clients should know what's being tracked, why, and how. That information builds a comfort zone for clients for accepting recommendations.
- To understand what counts or what's useful to try out, professionals have to understand both old and new media, and how they interact and can possibly reinforce each other.

- The job description in public relations has gone from order-taker to educator. Most users of this service don't recognize what options exist and their potential effectiveness and cost-efficiency.
- There are many variables, ranging from the client's objectives to the size of the organization, associated with what approach to use and how to measure results. Successful entrepreneurs may take stock of input-output-outcomes completely impressionistically.
- Trial-and-error is the only current way to get things done. Tracking can guide decision making about what approaches to embrace, when to let them go, and how to allocate or reallocate resources.

CHAPTER

INTERNET RISKS AND SECURITY

"For managing risk on the Internet, there is no ultimate solution."

—Mark Mershon

THE APPLICATIONS IN cyberspace are powerful. But you need to be very careful. Some people believe the Internet is a twenty-first-century version of the Trojan horse. Yes, this gift of digital technology has brought many benefits to business. That, of course, includes low-cost publishing, marketing, and public relations tools. In themselves, those digital options have significantly reduced the price of entry of starting enterprises in those fields. Anyone can buy a domain for $4.99 a year and learn how to design a website for free. Moreover, everyman and everywoman can become their own self-promoters, for their personal branding or their enterprises. Capitalists never had it so good.

RISKS IN CYBERSPACE

On the other hand, the technology that keeps the Internet interconnected is constantly mutating. That makes its users, no matter how technically astute they are, vulnerable to terrorism, cyberwar, spying, identity theft, fraud, file destruction, server collapse, intellectual property theft, leaking, e-mail that can be misinterpreted and lead to litigation, reputation damage, compromised privacy, spam, or worse.

The evil, the criminal, and the mere mischief-makers are not limited by geography or even cost. Simple technical know-how makes it possible for con artists in Germany to use a web server in the United States to steal the identity, including the credit card numbers, of a victim in Japan. Additionally, as cybercrime expert Robert Jones discusses in the 2006 book *Internet Forensics*, cybercrime has been globalized and is proliferating at an alarming rate as cyberfelons around the world view the Internet and its users as an easy mark for their ill-gotten gains.

Today, at least one billion individuals on this planet have access to the Internet—a number that keeps growing daily. Think about a country like India, which is now manufacturing laptops that can sell for an incredible $10! That represents a huge new population of potential victims.

These global miscreants are extremely clever and often devise ingenious ways to conceal their identities and their actual web addresses. Unfortunately, the authorities have not, as yet, devoted much time or resources to tracking down Internet swindlers. And when they are prosecuted, they usually walk away with light sentences. Looking ahead, one can be sure they will continue to ply their illegal trade as long as the money is there and the Internet available to make it possible.

Risk also comes from the Internet's free-speech and Wild West ethos. Currently, cyberlaw tends to default to protecting those who operate websites. For instance, under Section 230(c) of the Communications Decency Act of 1996, website operators have immunity from prosecution. Anyone posting illegal—often defaming—comments on a site can be brought to justice, but not easily, and the record shows that lawsuits won't get the plaintiffs much.

At least that is what Yale Law students Brittan Heller and Heide Iravani found out when they pursued justice against the anonymous posters making malicious false statements about them on AutoAdmit, a law school admissions discussion board. In a February 2009 article in *Portfolio*, "Slimed Online," David Margolick chronicles how the professional reputations of these two women were damaged when search engines picked up the comments, and yet the law was rarely on their side. That said, in August 2009, Google was ordered to give up the name of an anonymous blogger in another defamation case, which suggests that the debates and court challenges regarding this issue will probably continue for years to come.

In short, when it comes to the Internet, risk is everywhere, along with the benefits of this innovation. Mark Mershon, a former FBI assistant director, observes: "For managing risk on the Internet, there is no ultimate solution." Currently, Mershon is a senior consultant with The Dilenschneider Group. One project he's working on is helping to confront crime in the Caribbean, particularly gang violence. To Mershon, the bottom line for Internet use is: "Much of it is a judgment call. The convenience and reach are balanced with risk."

Admittedly, as technology matures, more safeguards—software, legislative, public education, grassroots backlash, and reputation-rehab services—become available to reduce the menace. Parents can monitor what their children view and block sites. Teachers educate minors about online predators. Virus protection software can prevent most of the invasions of networks and stand-alone computers. A whole new industry is emerging where companies can manipulate search engines to actually eliminate or at least lower the rankings of negative content. Today, enterprises such as ReputationDefender, eVisibility, Converseon, and 360i can also negotiate with site operators to erase certain items.

For now, however, the most basic advice is to know what you are doing. Know that the best defense is the offense. This chapter presents commonsense advice for protecting the nation, oneself, the family, and the company from the worst of the Internet.

TYPES OF MENACES

Internet security issues extend to national ones, such as intelligence and defense threats. Increasingly, actual war can be launched and fought in cyberspace. That's exactly what occurred between Russia and Estonia in 2007, when high-volume spam attacks brought down Estonian electronic systems.

There has been speculation that the massive summer blackout that hit the Northeastern and Midwestern United States and Ontario, Canada, in 2003 was triggered by Chinese hackers gaining access to the electrical grid system. According to the FBI, China is the primary originator of cyberattacks, with Russia and other Eastern European countries, and the Middle East, also high up on the list of defense risks.

Another kind of vulnerability is in the value of intellectual property. Other nations, competing companies, and one's own employees can steal proprietary information. The latter is increasingly likely as relationships between business owners and workers sour. This employee hostility is global. For instance, in Canada, the largest category of litigation involves labor disputes.

There are also myriad versions of what is called "malware." This is a type of software that is intentionally designed to destroy data on computers through deceptive means. Essentially they are Trojan horse programs with a limited payload that have the capability to bypass antivirus software.

Then there are those fake websites set up to look exactly like real company websites, such as those of banks. In this type of fraud, called "phishing," the process starts with an e-mail message directing the recipient to click on a URL that leads to the fake website. There, on the fake website, the visitor is misled into providing information ranging from a Social Security number to the PIN code for a bank debit card.

Spam, or unwanted e-mail, is another threat. Not only is it a nuisance, but it could have embedded in its attachment a virus or worm. Moreover, it can bring down a server. According to web security firm MessageLabs, more than 70 percent of e-mail is spam.

Misleading, fraudulent, and potentially dangerous communications can come in any and all types of digital packaging. Such schemes can range from the solicitation of information in exchange for supposed free gifts, to sales of discounted merchandise such as prescription medications that often never ship, to online predators seducing minors.

Of course, inadequately protected company trade secrets and research can lead to loss of intellectual property, disclosure of strategic plans, and access to confidential legal documents.

The e-mail risk keeps escalating. It is easy for e-mails to be leaked to the media by disgruntled employees. This is becoming commonplace with global reductions in force, cuts in benefits, and compensation reductions.

In addition, careless or even carefully worded e-mail communications have been retrieved and classified as "smoking guns" in litigation. There's more. The court requirement of gathering and interpreting e-mail during discovery can keep a company engaged in this process for years. The cost is enormous. Also, key personnel are usually taken away from operations to produce the e-mail.

Privacy of individuals can be compromised or destroyed by information that is disclosed and widely distributed online. Yale Law student Heide Iravani was stunned to read a family "secret" on AutoAdmit after a blogger dug up and posted a 1990s *Washington Post* article about a charge against the girl's father of using forged checks to purchase her a horse.

Any person, organization, brand name, product, service, or cause can be a target of "flaming" or deliberate and sustained attacks. High-profile entities are especially juicy targets.

ON THE OFFENSE

Playing defense is not an option. Rapid developments in technology will always work to the miscreants' advantage. They could have the edge. Moreover, never underestimate the power of their creativity. In his February 2009 *Portfolio Magazine* essay on Bernard Madoff titled "The Minus Touch," attorney/novelist Scott Turow wrote: "Crime is one of the least celebrated arenas of the human imagination."

Here are some fundamentals of going on the offense:

- Use old-fashioned common sense, recommends Mershon. Ask, "Do I trust this source?" Remember, the Internet is a high-risk zone. And anything that sounds too good to be true probably is not on the level.
- Put your own story out there and monitor reaction and where it comes from.
- Pursue the identification of cyberattackers. Let the results be known. That's a deterrent. As Jones warns, this is only a task for experts, not amateur sleuths. The case studies of these can be posted on websites and YouTube and perhaps become the script for television programs and films.
- Invest the time and money to select the most appropriate and effective software to detect and block viruses. This must be a work-in-progress. And it must extend to

wireless communications. Within your organization there must be a group dedicated to just this aspect of electronic communications. It won't be cheap. Consider that in terms of U.S. national security, some people estimate that detection and monitoring of digital threats could entail an expense of about $30 billion over a decade.

- Change access devices such as passwords or codes frequently. Investigate suspicious activity, including employees' and competitors' online movements. Prosecute to the fullest employees selling or leaking proprietary material. Litigate against illegal competitive actions. Here it isn't Internet law that is being applied. Therefore, litigation is a weapon that can and should be used.
- Investigate what services are the best fit for monitoring the Web for what is being said about business in general. This could be early warning of an attack. If bloggers are attacking the United Way, the Red Cross as well as its board members could be next.
- Have in place a plan for managing rumors and reputational crises. Sometimes no response is the right response. The mischief-makers, if they fail to get a rise out of the organization, could drop the matter and move on to another target. If a response is the answer, then have an overall message embedded in the response. That message might be that Company X has a sterling track record for global ethics. A message keeps the dialogue within boundaries. Never go off-message.

  As part of a response plan, set up a separate website or other digital spaces, such as blogs and microblogs, to manage your message. Enlist third parties to also use their sites to lend support. Never engage in a conversation on the opponents' electronic territories.
- Know the law, particularly about libel and defamation. Actually filing a lawsuit, or threatening to do so with a cease-and-desist order, has halted many a malicious amateur campaign. Most amateur attackers are clueless about the legal ramifications of what they are doing and will stop dead in their digital tracks when they are informed that they have broken the law.

- Maintain a strong web presence as a way to prevent or mitigate reputational attacks. Companies such as IBM enlist employees as bloggers. Since blogging is a free-flowing conversation, it tends to give the organization an aura of credibility: Here we are, ready to talk to you, with no filters. Another way is engaging constituencies through activities; for example, hold contests for user-generated input or encourage community building, promote suggestion sites, and provide links to information that's not easily available to customers.
- Hold confidential conversations in person, instead of using e-mail. Provided someone's office is private and isn't being bugged, why not just drop in on colleagues in person? On *The Sopranos*, Tony Soprano and Uncle Junior met in their medical doctor's office for powwows. Also, in this litigious era, e-mail is no medium for self-expression. To prevent the appearance of impropriety, keep functions such as marketing and research from exchanging e-mails. It's those supposed links that opposing lawyers look at.

When it comes to Internet use, there are real risks, but there's also the real danger of erring on the side of too much caution. That's a big mistake. The Internet has created fresh ways in which individuals and organizations can reach just about anyone, anywhere, for virtually no cost or low cost. Not doing that outreach makes for a competitive disadvantage.

TAKEAWAYS

- The Internet provides both benefit and risk. For that risk there is no ultimate solution. There probably never will be as long as the medium remains decentralized.
- Online threats involve national security, the value of intellectual property, employee sabotage, identify theft, fraud, and litigation because of e-mails, destroyed files, crashed servers, ruined reputations, and compromised privacy. Sometimes the dangers may be life threatening.

- Currently, technology, imagination, and the law are on the side of the miscreants. The only defense is to be on the offense.
- Proactive strategies and tactics include applying old-fashioned common sense; pursuing the identity of attackers; investing money and time to select menace-detecting software; frequently changing access codes; being up-to-date on Internet attack trends; having a rumor-management plan, including setting up digital sites for response; knowing the law; establishing a strong web presence; and exercising caution with e-mail.
- Not using the Web puts a business at a competitive disadvantage.

SECTION TWO

REACHING OUT

The five chapters in this section drill down into the actual practice areas of media relations, the trade press, employee communications, rumor management, and crisis communications. Here, the rubber meets the road. These chapters also explain ways in which off-line approaches can be used together with digital media.

Experimenting with mixing digital and traditional public relations strategies and tactics could be exciting—and fun. But for most digital immigrants, it's downright terrifying because, as German researcher Gerd Gigerenzer and his coauthors point out in their May 2009 digital edition of *Scientific American Mind*, "Individuals … have an emotional need for certainty."

In online communications, that need may never be met. The field always was, and always will be, about continual trial-and-error. That's because the medium of the Internet, unlike print or network broadcasting, undergoes rapid mutation with new digital applications emerging all the time. Consider how Twitter.com is already challenging the leading social network, Facebook.

What's required in experimenting with all these new entities is multiplied exponentially because digital strategies and tactics are themselves being commingled. What's the most effective way to reinforce a LinkedIn page with a podcast and webinar? That digital composite, in turn, could be tried out with conventional communications approaches. From such experimentation guidelines, tips, and insights can surely be derived. But there will be no fixed formulas as there have been for old media.

The next five chapters take both the new entrants to cyberspace and the more seasoned professionals, versed in more conventional media, by the hand. The experts who are sources for these chapters lead readers gently through the possibilities of creating fresh solutions for themselves and clients.

In some practice areas, such as investor relations and organizational communications, it is impossible to be relevant without applying digital strategies and tactics. In others, such as trade media and crisis communications, many of the principles or fundamentals remain the same, meaning those in charge of communications or the account can still supervise and succeed without hands-on experience in digital media.

But that, too, could change, quickly and radically. Already, not being a digital player is a competitive disadvantage for many communicators, no matter how prestigious their brand name and awesome their previous track record. Clients and prospects demand—or soon enough will demand—digital options. Increasingly, they are asking: "Will that media release be distributed via a blog, or will a video clip derived from it be shown on YouTube?" Or, "How does this agency conduct a virtual book tour, and how many of those online events have you done?"

Developing a digital mind-set for strategic planning and at least understanding the tools available for executing a digital strategy are becoming almost universal "must-dos." E-influence has also become a "must-know" for anyone who wants to survive in this technology-driven society. That's exactly why public libraries and other community outreach institutions are providing free or low-cost instruction in using the Internet.

The encouraging news is that once new digital immigrants venture into the promised land, they tend to not want to leave. That said, be prepared for "screen addiction" and, yes, regrets for avoiding digital for so many years or even months.

From these chapters, digital natives can also learn how to apply their raw knowledge of the Internet to unleash high-powered forms of advocacy, branding, research, information transmission, collaboration, fund-raising, and even selling. The altruistic and commercial possibilities of the Web are theirs, once they learn more about the ways of influence. They already know the basics and much more. Now, they can add on the value of influence, strategic thinking, and execution.

CHAPTER

MEDIA RELATIONS

"Now everything can be an opportunity. We can mix or not mix what are proven formulas in analog with experiments in digital. That means we can stick with mainstream media, only use them selectively to reinforce our message, or totally bypass them and rely on our own custom-made digital, audio, video, and even print distribution systems."

—SCOTT JOHNSON

THIS ERA COULD AND SHOULD be the best of times for media relations. As new media consultant Scott Johnson puts it: "Now everything can be an opportunity." However, that isn't the situation. Actually, for too many public relations representatives, it is the worst of times. That's because the simultaneous existence of what's been called "old media" and "new media," or "analog media" and "digital media," has generated misconceptions, fear, and lost jobs. As a result, there have been myriad missed opportunities when, as Johnson notes, everything should be an opportunity to be seized. For example, midsize companies operating on a shoestring could be blogging to test out global expansion and establish new contacts. But, not enough of them have been doing that.

This chapter deals with the options currently available in media relations. It explains how those options, together or as stand-alones, operate. It also assesses the potential risk and reward that go with applying hybrid strategies.

Why so much misunderstanding about media relations? Primarily, the confusion has come from the rigid stances on all sides. For instance, factions invested in analog media tend to discredit digital tone, content, and credibility. Then there are the factions trying to monetize digital media. That goal seems to appear to them to be easier if centralized media, owned by major corporations, would just disappear. Consequently, they write off what's coming from Time Warner and News Corp. and others as yesterday's news. No surprise, this battle of "ancients" and "moderns" has generated a media relations world of either/or, with elitist/populist versus expensive/low-cost.

REALITIES

Despite reduced revenue, reductions in force, and the questioning of their models, old media companies have not lost their influence. They probably never will. But no one knows what will happen or won't happen. What is known is that right now clients value, and often demand, being placed on *Larry King Live* and having their opinion-editorial in the print version of the *Wall Street Journal.*

In addition, approaches in old media are proven ones with fairly predictable outcomes. Moreover, face it, the centralized media companies control extraordinary money, power, and a web of well-placed contacts. Smart money bets on their remaking themselves into entities that fuse the best of analog traditions with ongoing digital innovation.

On the other hand, there is no question that new media ventures provide advantages of low-cost, built-in global reach, convenience, and youthful demographics. However, in new media, influence can fluctuate—rapidly. That's partly because the Internet operates differently. Not even the best hands-on digitals or the visionaries have figured it all out. Therefore, if the client is advised to establish a blog, create a video for YouTube, or do an e-mail blast, there are no guarantees that the client can expect certain results. In addition, because of the Wild West ethos of the online world, mutations are continual. What was effective yesterday may not be effective today. That adds up to this: Digital tools usually can only be applied and leveraged in a trial-and-error manner. Internet marketing leader Akin Arikan discusses that challenge in his book *Multichannel Marketing.*

Those accustomed to formulas yielding definite ballpark outcomes might be uncomfortable with the experimentation demanded by new media. There is also the personal or organizational branding issue. Some clients shun association with what they perceive to be renegades—digital sites such as DailyKos.com or an online crowd that communicates in 140 characters on Twitter.com. Do the chief executive officers of multinational corporations welcome the suggestion of placing their bylined articles on HuffingtonPost.com? Not so much. Media relations representatives could damage client relationships by making those kinds of recommendations.

CONVERGENCE

Can media relations be framed as something other than either/or? Yes. Instead of a binary universe, MIT media professor Henry Jenkins believes in a "convergence culture." Everything is changing, but nothing is really going away. For example, in his 2008 paperback *Convergence Culture: Where Old and New Media Collide*, Jenkins points to the once highly popular CBS show *Survivor* as old media configured for the Internet age. The format, he opines, was "designed to be discussed, dissected, debated, predicted, and critiqued." He contends not all media are created equally and currently the centralized folks have the resources—therefore, the power.

In the trenches of communications, the convergence is good news. New media consultant Johnson points out: "We can mix or not mix what are proven formulas in analog with experimentation in digital. That means we can stick with mainstream media, only use them selectively to reinforce our message, or totally bypass them and rely on our own custom-made digital, audio, video, and even print distribution systems."

Johnson came out of the newspaper business and migrated to the digital world. He understands both. "The problem with much of print," he argues, "is that the leadership didn't approach the Internet as the unique medium it is. They attempted to simply transfer analog tone and content onto a digital platform. A lot of them fell for unproven ideas by others—and implemented those ideas without really thinking about whether they actually attracted eyeballs or revenue."

Johnson also notes that during his newspaper days, he advised business leaders to "be concentrating on the handheld." That's because those devices are getting smarter and faster. That suggestion was dismissed in favor of "interactives" created for the big screen, with little or no consideration for screen size or software availability to the average user. They have not proven to be the answer yet.

Johnson is among those who believe that video and passive acceptance media are the future—people watching screens with little or no text and dynamic, beautiful visuals that work across cultures and language barriers.

THE MESSAGE—TESTING IT OUT

Debate about the future of media will continue. And it will be fascinating. However, what's necessary to know currently is how to use media options that are available.

Any outreach to media begins with crafting the message. In predigital organizations, executives and experts might have sat in conference rooms with high-priced research data spread over the table, brainstorming about what the message should be. That might still go on, at least where organizations can afford to invest so many expensive resources into shaping messaging. There is now an alternative.

Digital technology makes it possible to test out versions of the message without entailing expense. The cost, observes Johnson, "is in sweat equity and creativity. People need to remember—unless what you are doing will resonate with users on a personal level, don't bother. Gone are the days where value is attached to poorly created content. You have to invest in smart and creative people—and then let them do what they do. But there are still so many things to work out." That investment usually pays off.

Some people speculate that had John McCain, the 2008 Republican presidential candidate, experimented with his message of change, he might have discovered that components of his message about not voting for the other guy came across as negative. In a period where there was hunger for optimism, integrity, and joy, that negativity didn't resonate like the positive components of Barack Obama's change message.

One method of testing out the message is through blogs. Blogs have gone mainstream, and digital savvies rely on them for all kinds of research, including messaging. Key advantages of blogging include:

- Low or no cost
- Real-time message delivery
- Convenience
- Global reach
- Popularity

- Feedback through devices that measure traffic and pinpoint its source (e.g., comment sections, pickup and rankings by search engines, links coming in—particularly from influentials)

Here is an example of how an animal rescue organization went about messaging. Among the staff and volunteers, three themes seemed the most promising. They put them on three different blogs that had been operating about the same amount of time, had similar traffic patterns, and attracted the same search engines and links. Those three messages were:

- Rusty needs a home (with photo of dog).
- You need Rusty in your home (with photo of an empty living room).
- Your doctor recommends Rusty come home with you (with photo of an MD and a dog in a living room).

The staff and volunteers could have also used YouTube, podcasts, texting, social network sites such as Facebook, and banner ads on their own sites. In addition, they could have applied analog tactics such as press releases, booking guests on radio and TV programs, placing opinion pieces in newspapers, and polling. However, input from the blogs provided what they needed to know. The message that resonated the most was the one with the medical angle.

VERSIONS OF THE MESSAGE—TESTING THEM OUT

Once there is an overall message, there may or may not be this next step, which is experimenting with different versions of the message. Some prefer to have only one version of the message. Others have faith in producing diversity, with each version of a message giving the core message greater resonance. This latter approach is ideal when the message will be distributed through various media, ranging from case studies on the organization's website to appearances on late-night talk shows.

For a classic example of different versions of a message that fit together well to make an overall theme resonate, there are the creative efforts of Geico. The major initial message was: "Easy to deal with." The subordinate message was: "Save money, too." Three types of commercials were used just on the medium of television. Many viewers easily recall all three: the slick lizard with a Cockney accent; the drama-queen cavemen; the weird little pile of money.

If you decide to develop different versions of the message, the versions need to be tried out and the results assessed in the same way as the original message. Here is what to be alert for when designing the test and analyzing the results:

- Are the versions cannibalizing attention?
- Are they creating a mental mosaic in the minds and hearts of audiences?
- Are they neither cannibalizing nor reinforcing one another?

DISTRIBUTION—PROBABLY MORE TRIAL-AND-ERROR

Rolling out the message can mean more trial-and-error. In fact, a growing number of media representatives recommend mini-launches in many forms of media before a major launch. However, some organizations feel comfortable betting the ranch on one major roll-out from the get-go. They are usually the ones with generous budgets for promotions. Whatever the scope of the launch, factors to consider on choosing distribution vehicles include:

- *Audience.* Demographics determine everything. Clearly, to reach Millennials (also known as the net-generation and digital natives) with a message, digital tools are a must. The best tools are those used to start and build communities. Those communities should begin small until glitches can be ironed out. Then they can be promoted aggressively. To reach Generation X, baby boomers, and the silent generation (also known as digital immigrants), analog approaches are needed to anchor the message. If your target audience is mature women, for instance, start with placements of a story on *Oprah* or in *Family Circle* or on National Public Radio, and then move on to experimentation with digital tactics.

- *Time frame.* Urgency locks in decisions. A full-scale effort, despite any cost, is a must. Obviously, forget approaching monthly women's print media if they don't have continually updated online components. However, there are also zero-cost options such as e-mail blasts.
- *Budget.* Preparing an opinion-editorial for a top-tier daily print publication, or writing a feature article or case study for any trade outlet, print or digital, is expensive in terms of professional expertise needed to prepare copy and do the placement. The more shoestring the funding, the more digital vehicles make sense.
- *Manpower.* Are volunteers available to do grassroots digital communications? Then, there's no limit on what kinds of tactics can be used. Incidentally, as net-generation expert Don Tapscott notes in *Growing Up Digital*, when volunteers are allowed in and given the tools to transmit information and build communities, they create their own sources of influence.
- *Competition.* Your message may have to compete with other major news stories going on. That necessitates the use of more types of media and more creativity. During media coverage of the financial markets meltdown, space for other subjects was limited. Rule of thumb: Don't push your message if it won't fit on the radar screen. In most cases a message can be delayed and later reframed to appear fresh.
- *Network of contacts.* That's why establishment public relations firms are called in for handling high-stakes projects. They have existing relationships in all media, and their Rolodexes more or less guarantee results.
- *Talent.* Every aspect of selling to the media takes imagination. There's the story angle, compressing the message into buzzwords, headlining the pitch, arguing why audiences would find the story useful, and positioning the credentials

of the expert as unique. The less talent available the more effort expended with the least results obtained.

- *Stand-alone option.* Seasoned digitals have orchestrated whole campaigns relying only on their own blogs or microblogs. They can take advantage of the "relationship" they have already established with search engines, links that have become standard, and the ability to jump on opportunities such as breaking news.

SELLING—THE PROSPECT

The fundamentals of pitching a story are all about selling. Given clients' demands for placements in the decreasing number of old media outlets, some media representatives have decided to take sales seminars. They report significant improvement in their "sales" performance.

In essence, the selling process covers everything from what is being hawked (that is, the contents of the story) to how it's being positioned and packaged. These principles apply whether the pitch is directly to the audience of a stand-alone site or to the editorial page editor of the *New York Times*.

In selling, the top-three musts are: 1) Focus on the prospect, not oneself. For that you must 2) know who those prospects are, what they want and need, and who their competition is, and 3) know who else is approaching them.

When targeting a niche audience online—for instance, owners of aging dogs—it is fairly simple. That's why niche marketing, or what digital expert Chris Anderson, editor in chief of *Wired* magazine, calls "the long tail," is so effective. There isn't a lot to know. Most digital sites are niches.

When approaching a publisher, editor, producer, or talk show host, the first step in research is to become familiar with that person's publication, site, or show. Each has a distinct personality. That personality is bound to change, somewhat or radically, when the leadership changes. That's why trade media such as

Mediabistro.com and Odwyerpr.com issue continual updates on who's going and who's coming. In the 1990s, when Tina Brown came to the *New Yorker*, she revolutionized the tone and content from upper-crust intellectual to more yuppie pop culture.

Part of this "getting acquainted" is to find out what has already been covered recently. If *Vanity Fair* just ran a major spread on power brokers under age 40 working at think tanks, it won't be in the market for another piece like that anytime soon. Also, find out if the outlet has an editorial calendar that specifies special upcoming issues that may focus on a theme such as design, MBA programs, or divorce.

Then find out what the media outlet's competition is doing. You'll open an editor's or producer's ears if you can say, "*Vogue* recently carried a mediocre, incomplete spread on plus-size clothes. My client can provide you with sources, photos, and insider information for far better coverage." Media are fiercely competitive with one another.

Also remember that media decision makers are human beings. They want to be recognized for their influence, power, and public service. Some organizations have even chosen to honor them, if appropriate, with awards or fellowships for study. It also makes good networking sense, occasionally, to send them an e-mail on the productive controversy that one of their articles or commentaries generated. Also, it's standard in media relations to provide tips, early warning of news to break, background information, and access to clients.

Of course, it's useful to pitch to those who are more likely to buy. They could be local access cable programs, weeklies, start-ups, and media known for using lots of outside content. Media directories such as *Bacon's* and *Leadership* provide descriptions of the many markets that exist for print, digital, audio, and visual outlets, complete with contact information. Print volumes of these directories are revised periodically, with an online component available as well for accessing updates to listings.

SELLING—THE GOODS

Success in media relations involves the judgment to know what can be sold and how, and what won't sell, no matter how many bells and whistles are attached. The trick is to communicate that assessment to a client, partner in a firm, or cofounder of an enterprise before pitching. And it is the job of the PR practitioner to frame the pitch in the most compelling and attention-getting manner.

Salable goods require:

- *Something of interest or newsy, at least to a target market.* That can be reinforced by copying, pasting, and forwarding a blog post on the topic that was picked up by *Wired* or *Fast Company,* for example, and attracted thirty comments. Media people listen to other media people.
- *A public service angle.* Nothing should appear to be self-serving; rather, it must add to the common good.
- *The right timing.* A piece on how to recycle Christmas cards isn't going to sell to a daily in the summer. A topical angle can mean a sure and quick sale.
- *Material that isn't easily available elsewhere.*
- *Fresh sources.* If Joe has been quoted in ten articles after being laid off, an editor doesn't want to be number eleven on the list.
- *Integrity.* The requirements here extend from an authentic voice to adequate documentation of any assertions made in the pitch.
- *Exclusivity.* That's why a story is pitched as an exclusive to one outlet at a time.
- *Credentials of the sources being interviewed or quoted and their track record in media.* These should be described briefly and any books or published materials by the sources sent via FedEx.

SELLING—THE PITCH

In parts of the highly competitive film industry, the way ideas are pitched is known as a "high concept." What could wind up as a 120-minute movie is captured in a sentence. Analogies are frequently used to do the heavy lifting. A high-concept pitch for a film about a disabled Jewish woman who brings peace to the Middle East might be: "Female Jewish Forrest Gump shuts down war in the Middle East."

High concept serves to communicate a story and theme or lesson in a brief, catchy format. Some people call that approach "stickiness," or creating ideas that attract and keep attention. In this era of short attention spans, short and punchy are requirements for the title of the proposal, as well as for the e-mail pitch/phone call, the lead sentence, and all the rest of the content that tells why the media would be interested. If the pitch is continually rejected, ask colleagues for copies of their successful pitches that resulted in placements. Analyze them. Imitate the model.

Often well-crafted pitches don't work because the content just isn't marketable, at least not in its initial form. Content can be reconfigured by trying new angles. That can come from providing a topical hook (everyone needs a gimmick), conducting original research or polling, accessing research, providing information or insights that aren't widely known, or changing the tone to perhaps humor or satire.

Given the instant feedback available in blogging, media representatives can quickly gain experience with myriad approaches to headlines, lead sentences, amount of supporting evidence, and tone. A few weeks of that kind of basic training could be called Pitching 101. After completing just such an informal crash course in pitching, one writer/blogger, who only occasionally did publicity, placed most of the stories she pitched.

Those still not succeeding in pitching their stories can ask others working in digital media for candid input on how to close the deal. Folks working in digital media and online seem to be more accessible than those in the analog world. Perhaps it's because digital communication is at its core a conversation.

COURSE CORRECTION

In the days when the powers-that-be assumed the role of infallibility, course correction was usually avoided. That's because a change would concede that mistakes had been made. In a world that has become so uncertain and where relationships have become flat versus top-down, course correction is more acceptable. In some disruptive industries, such as search technology, failure is considered a necessary rite of passage. However, common sense should rule. If so many mistakes are being made, then maybe those making the mistakes should get the boot.

When is it acceptable to change a message? Sometimes the times change, as when a new administration comes to Washington, D.C., and the old message no longer resonates. Then, testing out fresh approaches is mandatory.

When is it acceptable to change how the message is distributed? Usually when the individual or the organization transforms itself. Actually, one approach here is to use different kinds of media. In the final laps of Campaign '08, McCain could have done that more effectively—and quickly. A muckraking group might seek to attract establishment support by publishing a commentary in the *Financial Times* or *Forbes*.

As with everything else in human affairs, no one welcomes too much change. Therefore, it's wise to take the time at the outset to get the message right and the distribution system humming smoothly.

TAKEAWAYS

- Hardened stances about so-called old and new media have created needless confusion about blending both in media relations.
- Centralized media outlets still retain considerable influence and power.
- Digital media outlets continue to struggle to monetize what they produce.

- New media tactics require trial-and-error.
- Digital sites are not an appropriate fit for every client.
- Low-cost digital technology allows testing of the message and can help determine the approach to distribution before embarking on a major campaign.
- Choice of distribution vehicles depends on audience, time frame, budget, manpower, talent, competing stories, and the network of contacts.
- Pitching is a sales process, extending from the goods to be hawked (the content) to how the deal is closed (positioning and packaging).
- Rejection can come from poorly designed pitches or an uninteresting contact. Both factors can be remedied.
- Advice is frequently available in digital media.
- Course correction is acceptable, but should be done in moderation.

CHAPTER

TRADE MEDIA

"By definition, 'trade media' are disposed to providing publicity for the 'trade,' be that construction, law, autos, medicine, or pet food."

—JOEL POMERANTZ

"TRADE MEDIA" IS AN UMBRELLA TERM—and a sprawling one—that covers print (newspapers, magazines, newsletters), online, audio, and video material about specific industries and professions. This is a broad category, and thanks to digital technology, expanding rapidly.

For example, print publications such as *Active Trader* or *Sales & Marketing Management* were generally classified as trade media in the past. They are distributed by regular ("snail") mail and sold in bookstores and on newspaper stands. Revenues to support them primarily came from advertising. In addition, the commercial enterprises publishing the trade publication might have other profit centers that could include industry-related special events, trade shows, and conferences.

TYPES OF TRADE MEDIA

Typically, trade media can be local in circulation (*Crain's Chicago Business*), statewide (*North Carolina Builder*), regional (*Southern Jewelry News*), or national (*National Underwriter*). The vast majority of key trade media are, in fact, national.

As to frequency, they can be published daily (*Aviation Daily*), weekly (*Travel Weekly*), bimonthly (*Drug Topics*), or monthly (*Modern Plastics*).

But in all cases, the focus is usually a niche one. The parameters might be law or the retail grocery business, for instance. That niche orientation is what keeps trade media so influential.

Because of the nature of digital technology, which keeps generating communications hybrids, trade media have become fluid.

There are all sorts of permutations on the old print publication that came out regularly and arrived in snail mail.

One is the mixture of print and online vehicles, such as what J. R. O'Dwyer Company, Inc., does. Another permutation may not even start out as trade media. It might be an online community for mothers that, because of its popularity, becomes a must-be-part-of site for certain professions. Eventually those larger companies take it over, usually through buying the site. There are also stand-alone blogs such as AboveTheLaw.com, which gain such clout in the legal profession that they become more influential in certain circles than official trade media such as the *ABA Journal.*

Trade media cover whatever matter to those in business and professions. But there is no predicting how this category will mutate in the future. The audiences for trade media are diverse. In fact, it is not accurate to classify this category as solely business-to-business. One type of reader is the person whose business or profession is directly involved. The chief executive officer of Ford, his supply chain, and competitors probably read *Motor Age.* But so might automobile enthusiasts, hobbyists, and perhaps even regulators in federal, state, and local government. However, the tone and content are directed to the trade. The type of article in *Motor Age* would never appear in a strictly consumer publication like *Family Circle.*

WIDE OPEN FOR PUBLICITY

For business professionals, there is no better place to go for publicity than the trade media. "By definition, trade media are disposed to reporting on business and the professions," points out Joel Pomerantz, a principal at The Dilenschneider Group. "That is their reason for existence. This is very different from purely consumer-oriented media."

But dealing with trade media still requires doing one's homework. Placing announcements, feature stories, opinion-editorials, and case studies in a trade outlet entails understanding each publication, site, or community.

Each vehicle has its own personality. Therefore, each has to be analyzed in order to match the format, tone, and content. Material submitted to the *ABA Journal* would be positioned and packaged differently than it would if it were being submitted to AboveTheLaw.com.

Also, each has its preferred ways of being contacted and doing business. For most, the go-to person is the editor. Some editors want completed copy sent by e-mail. Some want to be queried first—by e-mail. Others accept queries by phone. Some have specific guidelines for a query. Certain kinds of graphics and photos may be required.

There are different lead times depending on whether the publication is a daily, weekly, monthly, or even quarterly. In addition, some trade publications have editorial calendars. For a computer trade pub, April could be the edition covering social online media. Those planning placements should know this schedule.

How can placement representatives find out the ins and outs of trade media? That information is available in a number of ways. The publication's website might contain guidelines for submission. There are also directories that provide comprehensive, detailed briefings. One is *Bacon's Magazine Directory.* That franchise has both print manuals and online components that are updated constantly. Another way to get the scoop is to network with those who have placed content in trade media. Since many trade publications have small staffs that may turn over frequently, it is imperative to make sure that recommendations passed along by the network are current.

VALUE

Despite the diversity in trade media, Pomerantz cites several distinct ways in which they create value for an overall publicity plan:

- Trades publish or broadcast industry-specific and professional material that mainstream media might not. That includes personnel changes, office relocations, awards, anniversaries, product launches or upgrades, executive-bylined commentary and features, case studies, success stories, social responsibility initiatives, and legislative analysis. It is simply "easier" to get these items in the trade press than in any other type of media. These materials can also be recycled as reprints for all kinds of constituencies, ranging from employees to prospects.

- Trade publications are read by media and financial analysts. Journalists and Wall Street analysts make a point of monitoring the leading trades of the industries or professions they cover. Having an item published in the trade press could be an indirect way of gaining access to these influentials. The strategy here is to work the way up from the "minors" to the "majors." However, in certain sectors, a report in an influential trade outlet can be viewed as just as important, if not more so, than one in the mainstream media. Prominent examples are *Variety* (entertainment industry), *Women's Wear Daily* (fashion industry), and *Ad Age* (advertising and promotion).
- Customers and clients, conditioned by the Internet to dig for information and perspective, also monitor the trades.
- Trades provide opportunities to attach a human face to an overall company or professional message (for example, efficiency through supply chain management or certain aspects of technology) that may otherwise appear detached.
- The trade media sometimes sponsor trade shows, conferences, and panels in which to participate.
- Trade publishing can be tied into issue-oriented and/or product advertising. Online, these tie-ins can be part of a search engine optimization campaign.

ACCESS

Many of the same recommendations for placements in general media also apply to the trade media. All media outlets are, after all, in a competitive arena, vying for circulation numbers or page views, advertising revenues, citations by other media, hyperlinks, and must-read status. The best approach is to take advantage of whatever will help the media outlet achieve these goals. That's common sense, of course. Here are more specific suggestions:

- Develop relationships with the publisher, editors, and journalists. At a minimum, that involves being a regular reader or visitor to their sites. For instance, an e-mail can be sent about a particularly useful article or a comment posted on a blog, with links to the site's content. At their best, publicists provide backgrounders, breaking news, off-the-record information, and gossip to the trades. They make their executives available for briefings and quotes.
- Pitch as many exclusives as possible. Of course, press releases about product launches, recalls, and personnel announcements will be distributed on a mass basis, which means all the trades receive them simultaneously. Moreover, the trades should receive every general release, if just as a courtesy. But other, less-general material should be offered to only one publication or site at a time.
- Pitch the way the publication or site prefers. The rules can sometimes be broken, but not too often.
- Position and package the pitch with a tentative, catchy title, topical tie-ins, brief summary of main points, evidence of controversy, and explicit reasons readers will find the topic useful. Attach any documents that will help close the deal. Those might be other media coverage on the topic, a book that's already been written and published by the author of the bylined feature you submit, or security analysts' coverage.
- Be prepared to purchase advertising. This helps keep the publisher, editors, and journalists in their jobs.
- Discuss opportunities to participate in trade shows, conferences, and panels. Nail down specifics about what media, companies, and consumers will be there.
- Book speakers for trade-sponsored special events. A formal proposal is frequently required. The proposal needs to spell out the speaker's credentials and particular angle on a subject. It would also indicate how the trade could derive ancillary

benefits because the speaker would ensure media coverage and a certain number of attendees.

LEVERAGING MOMENTUM

Media pay attention to media. Once the topic appears in the trades, a platform is provided to gain publicity for the story (or the leader authoring the story) with other media and other constituencies. So you are working from a position of strength.

One traditional technique is getting permission from the trade to have reprints made of the article or story that was published and distributing it as an attractive glossy via snail mail. Reprint rights also allow for electronic distribution.

A less conventional approach is to leverage the trade coverage itself as a way to penetrate general media. For instance, being published in the trade media could be the best indirect path to reaching consumers who read *Vanity Fair* or business leaders who read the *Wall Street Journal.* How? The publicist can copy, paste, and e-mail the clip with a catchy title and short cover note discussing another possible angle. The message, of course, is: Another branch of media, noncompetitive to you, found this newsworthy; you might, too. The copy, paste, e-mail approach can also be used to book clients for appearances on radio and television talk shows.

BEING THE TRADE MEDIA

A blog is not a trade publication as the term is commonly understood. But in this digital age, you can exploit the opportunities afforded online to create a blog as a valuable, related outlet to serve the interests of a particular company or professional firm.

For example, the plaintiffs' law firm Marler Clark operates multiple blogs related to food-borne diseases. The content ranges from background material to breaking news. It's been said that because of the effectiveness of this outreach, Marler Clark "owns" this niche in law. Since the online postings serve as a search engine optimization mechanism, Marler Clark usually gets top rankings in searches. Through search engine optimization, smaller businesses have also found producing their own blogs to be an effective and low-cost marketing approach.

Remember, the world of digital media is not a zero-sum game the same way analog is. Hyperlinks among media provide incentive for all media to pull in the same direction to promote stories. To be sure, there is still the goal of having an exclusive or being the one that breaks the news. But even that is becoming less relevant to influence as simply being part of the conversation.

More and more professional-services firms have company-wide or agency-wide blogs in which all the partners or principals contribute commentary, discuss research, and provide mini case studies. It's an efficient way to potentially reach constituencies around the globe, as well as a launching platform from which to pitch to the media, trade and general.

Here are some basics for setting up a blog to become part of the trade media:

- Have a clear message formulated about what you are supposed to be communicating. For example: "Management Consultant X is the thought leadership brand in supply chain management," or "Public Affairs Y provides access to world leaders." Everything goes back to the message.
- Explore through trial-and-error what niche focus is most effective in transmitting the message. For example, several blogs can be launched in a low-profile manner. The one that resonates, that seems to create buzz with the right audience, will be the one to pursue.
- Educate participants about the value created by this outreach. Train them in the "tricks" of gaining, keeping, and growing audiences online.
- When ready for prime time, promote the blog. An indirect way is to invite people outside the organization to contribute.
- Monitor traffic to determine what's working. Do more of that. Do continual course correction to eliminate what's not working.

- Consider turning the blog into a profit center. That could involve selling advertising, sponsoring paid special events, and spinning off services and products. It might also mean creating a center for coaching others on how to set up their own trade media.

TAKEAWAYS

- *Trade media* is a broad term referring to myriad kinds of communications vehicles focused on a specific industry or profession. That niche coverage is the source of the trade media's influence.
- Placements in trade media provide a platform for reaching other constituencies, including general media, from a position of strength.
- The basics about building relationships with publishers, editors, and journalists in general media are essentially the same for trade media.
- From experience with official trade media, it's possible to experiment with establishing your own blog. That experience in turn could morph into a profit center.

CHAPTER

ORGANIZATIONAL COMMUNICATIONS

"The goal in organizational communications is to align the employees with the company's vision, values, and business strategy so that both the individual employee and the company are more successful."

—Jonathan Dedmon

LIKE THE INTERNET ITSELF, employee or organizational communications (OC) can be made to do whatever needs to get done. As tools, they are completely open-ended. And, thanks to digital technology, OC's scope, reach, and results are exploding. The function has become critical in a business environment where the traditional models and assumptions are crumpling. Leaders now look to OC to help the company or institution survive and eventually wind up thriving. At the time this handbook was being written, survival was the immediate global business goal, as well as the individual professional one.

For that reason, currently OC are used, according to Jonathan Dedmon, a principal with The Dilenschneider Group, "to strengthen employees' commitment to their respective companies and their companies' goals." Another way of putting that is that the OC role has become the in-the-moment playing field. Depending on what happens there, a future may or may not be in the cards.

After the dot.com collapse in the early twenty-first century, Cisco might have not been able to survive and wind up a stronger company without its OC. Since then, OC experts routinely monitor what Cisco has been doing. An earlier example was IBM during its mid-1990s turnaround. Before that, there was the Iacocca-led turnaround at Chrysler, which, some contend, represented a revolution in OC, both internal and external.

EMPLOYEE/COMPANY—BROADER DEFINITION

Dedmon points out that the definitions of both employee and company have become rather broad.

"Employee" is a term with a specific definition for legal purposes. However, in more general uses, those referred to as employees could hold full-time positions with benefits or part-time positions with no benefits. They can be those at a law firm who are encouraged to take a one-year unpaid sabbatical until demand picks up. Or they can be entry-level management consultants whose start dates are delayed six months while new business is being developed. Contractors are sometimes called "freelance employees," but usually they do not consider themselves as such, nor does the organization. There may be a written contract involved, but it will not turn a freelancer into a person with the responsibilities and rights of someone the law defines as an "employee."

The "company" could include not only the organization, but its entire supply chain, joint-venture partners, and even customers who, in these digital times, might collaborate with the company to create brands. Cisco includes customers in its OC. The "company" might even open its intranet or password-only blog to special guests such as select media or favored government officials. Back around 2004, Chrysler gave such access to key reporters, which was perceived as a perk—and a prestigious one.

OC can be conducted 24/7. The communications may be in person, one-on-one, in a group, in print, delivered digitally (including to mobile devices), or even video (including YouTube) and audio productions.

THE OLD INTERNAL COMMUNICATIONS

The current OC function has evolved significantly since the days when it was primarily referred to as employee or internal communications. Back then, its role was essentially to transmit information, top-down and one-way, from management to workers. The function produced and distributed the glossy house organ, handbook, description of benefits, videos, speeches, announcements on bulletin boards, direct mail sent to employees' homes, and inserts in paychecks, and would also oversee special events such as awards ceremonies.

That was then. That "then" was a time of relative stability within companies and in the external business environment. From the end of World War II until the late 1970s, change didn't characterize the operation of business. In fact, companies were rewarded by Wall Street for maintaining predictability in sales, revenues, and profits.

If there was too much revenue that could be classified as profits, the powers-that-be made sure that money was spent on dividends, advertising, or a new employee benefit before the books were closed. There wasn't much that had to be explained to workers. And since the social contract included career security and a company-funded pension, workers were content enough not to ask too many questions.

Perhaps because of that passivity, says The Dilenschneider Group's senior consultant and investment relations expert Joseph A. Kopec, "The old model of internal communications was based on the assumption that human beings are rational and behave rationally." Kopec believes that model has been totally discredited. The factors involved in the global financial unraveling have reinforced the idea that humankind is predisposed to be anything but rational. To be effective, OC strategists have to uncover what, in self-absorbed irrational human beings, drives people to work together for a collective goal. They have the difficult job of figuring out how to create a collective "we" among workers to get them to cooperate. Recall that even Communism wasn't effective in superimposing that mind-set on mankind.

GLOBALIZATION AND TECHNOLOGY

The old model of internal communications crumpled, of course. It had to. By the late 1970s business became global and driven by technology. To survive, companies had to become smart and creative about motivating workers without the carrots of job security and a nice pension. Also, the world's love affair with the "corporation," narrated so well by management guru Peter Drucker, hit a wall.

One of the brightest and most imaginative of companies committed to survival has been consumer electronics retailer Best Buy, which has not only survived but put its competitor Circuit City out of business.

Best Buy's own employees invented a totally multipurpose, digital interactive mechanism called The Watercooler. As Internet specialist Don Tapscott explains in his 2009 book *Growing Up Digital*, The Watercooler facilitates:

- Direct means of communications among all levels in all locations. The system is porous.
- Communication that is all-inclusive. The system disseminates basic information, questions asked and answered about products, competitive positioning, how-tos for installation, brainstorming ideas, and input about decisions to be made.
- Informal, wiki-style collaboration on formal projects.

The direction of Best Buy digital communications runs across the organization, not top-down. The tone can be serious, satiric, or agitated. The content is not polished and massaged by the powers-that-be. As Reena Jana reports in *BusinessWeek* (March 12, 2009), this approach could be adopted by other companies that now rely heavily on employees for innovation, both for the ideas and the execution.

However, globalization and technology have made profitability too uncertain for any company to anoint one approach as "the best practice" and stick with it. Best Buy itself has had a rough patch. So has Cisco. Cisco's approach to open-network communications that include customers was featured as *Fast Company*'s January 2009 cover story.

That's exactly why OC strategists continue to struggle to find what gets results today, not yesterday, and what works for their own company, not at some other company. Yahoo!, for example, has returned to top-down management, which means more old-line-type communications. Apple remains secretive, not transparent. IBM seems to have a hybrid approach, relying on many employee bloggers, but also the controlled messaging of a huge organization. A major challenge during the transition from start-up to public company involves formalizing the communications: to go from a free-for-all to a system that can ensure the confidentiality required by SEC rules, protect intellectual property, and manage leaks by employees unhappy with the change.

No, one size does not fit all. And what fits today may be an impediment tomorrow.

FUNDAMENTALS

There are fundamentals in OC that apply in all settings. They include:

- *Knowing who the audience is.* It probably isn't homogeneous. The workplace is increasingly diverse in terms of racial, national, and ethnic identification; sexual orientation; and generation. Within each category of diversity, such as generation, there are also differences. Baby boomers, for one, aren't a monolith, neither is the net-generation. What they probably share are common values related to work. Both quantitative and qualitative research can uncover those shared sacred cows. Those are the "keep" points of leverage. The ideal research mechanism, in terms of achieving high participation and yielding insight, is the anonymous e-survey.
- *Establishing trust.* Trust is everything. Although it can be achieved in an infinite number of ways, the trick is to build it in ways that seem authentic to the organization. It could be a fatal error in judgment to force-fit language and actions that may have created trust in other organizations. Moreover, trust building is always a work-in-progress. Usually, it starts with the first-line supervisor, to whom most workers look for candid information, even if it's bad news. Daily, by words, body language, facial expressions, and actions, a supervisor can gain or lose trust. The *actions* part is key. Employees monitor what the higher-ups do, not so much what they say.
- *Listening.* Listening breaks open hearts and minds. All human beings want to feel a sense of belonging. That comes when they sense they are being heard, not necessarily agreed with.

How can organizations listen? Through intranets, e-surveys, regular meetings (even though management and workers complain about meetings, they want that communal experience), town meetings in which the presentation is short and the dialogue long, relatively easy access to all levels, and frequent executive visits to all locations. At one major auto supplier, the chief executive officer famously managed to alienate those whose support he needed most by consistently not listening.

- *Being human.* A human face trumps a corporate persona. Human doesn't necessarily mean folksy, familiar, or cool. Not every leader can or should be another Warren Buffett. All it takes is presenting oneself as real enough to connect with another human being. The Organization Man and the Professional Woman have become anachronisms in this digital age. Business has become a conversation, even if that conversation is framed as top-down, with ever so few questions allowed. Did a former, much-publicized, high-tech executive fail because of her old-line image of extreme professionalism?
- *Offering meaningful messages.* Positive and negative news should be positioned as equal and as meaningful. Everyone knows that stuff happens. What counts is that when news, good or bad, is released it's in the form of a message. All news is a platform for a message. News is never presented in isolation. People long for meaning. They need it. A message embeds meaning into the raw data, event, or incident, minimizing uncertainty and ambiguity.
- *Being specific—and entertaining.* Employees need to know how their particular job and their function fit with the corporate plan. Once they know that, they can come up with ideas on how to do their job or function better or cheaper or faster. That fit can be communicated through narratives, role-playing, humorous videos with scripts composed by employees, daily e-mail blasts, and a wiki. Distributing the corporate plan in isolation isn't enough.
- *Delivering more with less.* Even when companies find that employees want frequent communications, they also find that communications have to be framed for short attention spans.

Simplify the concept, and put it into easy-to-read language. Use lots of white space, and perhaps some graphics. Break up a complex topic into a number of simpler topics and distribute those communications one by one, not as a massive e-communication.

- *Choosing the right medium.* The right medium means the message will be communicated. The wrong medium means no transmission. Audiences may want the message wrapped in comic-book graphics, not wordy prose. Or they might be print holdouts who prefer the inverted pyramid style of writing they learned in Freshman Composition. If there are diverse cultures and generations in the workplace, something for everyone might have to be provided, on a rotating basis.
- *Celebrating group accomplishments, not individual ones.* Creating a "we" ethos will happen. The force of organizational pressure can transform even the most self-absorbed person into a team member. That's the upside of being in a survival mode. Desperation can be a powerful bonding force.
- *Making a commitment to measurement.* Always measure. But first the OC folks have to decide what counts and how to count it. That's tricky. Participation in the intranet may be 97 percent, but profits continue to decline. Workers might have an 87 percent comprehension of the fit between their jobs and the corporate plan, but numbers for productivity, quality, and safety are down. OC leaders are not alone in dealing with this issue. As our economy continues to change, every discipline is hitting a wall on what to measure, what tools to use to do that measurement, and how to interpret results. According to eMarketer, in 2009, and just in the United States alone, advertisers will likely spend more than $25 billion on display ads. But that growth could be impeded because of lack of reliable data about how many eyeballs the ads reach.

MISCHIEF-MAKERS

With so much abrupt change, especially reductions in force, a growing problem for OC leaders is how to manage those who might be referred to as "mischief-makers." In a less volatile marketplace, they would quit or not risk stirring up trouble. That's the way it used to be when lifetime security was a possible career goal. Now, those same workers often see themselves as having too much to lose by resigning or not much to lose by leaking internal communications or agitating coworkers. Organizations need not feel shamed if they are facing this kind of tension and conflict. It's simply another sign of the times.

Some guidelines:

- *Expect leaks.* They go with an insecure workforce. They can be reduced by strong internal relationships, especially between the immediate supervisor and the staff. But leaks can't be entirely prevented. That means all memos, announcements, performance reviews, and even celebratory notices must be composed with the media, the mainstream, and cyberspace in mind. Showing a little heart will go a long way. If the material leaked has an uncaring tone, it usually gets the most negative attention. Use of *corporatese* is not far behind in terms of bringing a negative reaction.
- *Establish a mechanism, such as an anonymous intranet, for releasing pent-up steam and emotions.* This kind of mechanism also provides employee input about what others are thinking and feeling. Create guidelines for use. If this sort of open vehicle is monitored for profanity, threats, and undue hostility, the organization should be able to keep it reasonable and under control.
- *Transmit any information that might be easily misquoted or misinterpreted on a one-to-one basis, in person.* That leaves no trail—paper or electronic. It turns the situation of "he/she said" into "I said." Miscreants understand that without evidence any charges or complaints they make won't fly; they have no information to use against the company.
- *Neutralize counterforces with gestures of inclusion.* This is an old-fashioned organizational tactic. Appoint the chief gossip to head up a project on leveraging the grapevine to stop silo thinking, or appoint the leading dissident shareholder to the

board of directors. These are the people who love the power and prestige. This tactic also avoids their suing the company if they are terminated or demoted at some future date.

- *Get the facts out.* When negative activity escalates, it is frequently a signal that members of the organization are experiencing insecurity, alienation, or downright panic. Find out what their fears are and address them. If there is fear about job loss, be candid with the facts as they are known. Promise more facts when they are available. Keep that promise. Answers fill black holes of uncertainty and help to calm anxiety, which will in turn help return organizational confidence. Harvard Business School professor Rosabeth Moss Kanter identified confidence (in her 2004 book of that title) as the key factor in management winning streaks. The lack of it can put in motion a losing streak or prevent an organization from overcoming one.
- *Bust up bunkers.* Groups at all levels will attempt to hide. Forcing them back into the organizational mainstream reinforces the "we" ethos. Peer pressure can emerge against the mischief-makers.
- *Celebrate milestones, such as a return to profitability, and share the rewards throughout the organization.* Symbolism is a powerful communications tactic.

STARTING OVER

"Do we really have to start over on how we communicate internally?" That's what organizations in trouble frequently ask Kopec. To get at the answer, the first step is to identify the communications effort's weak or nonexistent links, as well as its strengths. This can be done through an e-survey on the intranet as well as with focus groups, conducted by third parties, querying randomly selected employees whose identities are kept confidential, and by observing.

What's not effective is experimenting in a low-key way with too many approaches. Forget systematizing anything. What counts is finding out what messages resonate and how to best position, package, and distribute them. The less macro-thinking OC leaders are, the more results they will probably get.

TAKEAWAYS

- OC helps companies survive—and positions them to thrive. There are numerous examples, ranging from Cisco in the early twenty-first century to IBM back in the mid-1990s and Chrysler in the early 1980s. But keep in mind that effective OC, however well executed, does not prevent performance setbacks, such as Cisco and Best Buy have experienced.
- No one size fits all. OC must be custom-made for the company culture and the current threats and opportunities.
- The fundamentals of OC, which help ensure success, really represent common sense.
- Mischief-makers can be managed.
- Every organization has strengths. They have to be identified and leveraged. Weak communications links have to be replaced.

CHAPTER

RUMOR MANAGEMENT

"When rumors persist, we have to ask: 'What do the people behind those rumors really want?'"

—Jim Wieghart

IN ESSENCE, "RUMOR" IS speculation about what was, is, or could be. It may be accurate or a base canard. The speculation could be well substantiated, as when investigative journalists have informed sources for an emerging story. It could be created and passed on without any substance. That's frequently the sometimes creative mischief of youth or those with agendas. There is the speculation that has some relation to reality, but the question is how much. The research of psychologist Nicholas DiFonzo found that many work-related rumors turn out to be true.

Rumors exist for a wide variety of reasons. They go back to biblical times. Mankind needs them. The only thing new is that today we have digital communications to help disseminate rumors more quickly and globally.

FUNCTIONS OF RUMORS

Everyone has been sucked into the force field of a rumor. It's a universal experience. Often, people are just trying to appear to know more than they actually do. They rely on rumors for that sense of control. During periods of change, rumor activity usually increases. Early researchers in this field, psychologists Gordon Allport and Leo Postman, found that the more unknowns in the situation, the stronger the rumors could be.

Sometimes, rumors are deliberately planted to get input on how a proposal might be received. That's common in politics when leaders are considering introducing a bill or appointing someone to a high post. This is a stealth way of ferreting out public opinion, assessing a national or local mood, and estimating support.

Engaging in this tactic is commonly known as "leaking." Leaking is a standard practice in lines of work that involve volatility, perception, and media attention.

Other times, rumors are strategic weapons to use against the opposition, a competitor, or an enemy. In old Hollywood, the classic statement to circulate was about an actor's sexuality, as in someone's gay or is a party to extramarital affairs. Those rumors might or might not be true.

In addition, rumors can be devices to influence or manipulate events such as stock market movements for personal gain. That's easily accomplished in the era of the Internet, given all the bulletin boards, chat rooms, blogs, and microblogs available to market manipulators. Consider the rumors about the health of Apple's CEO Steve Jobs. By the time the company denied the rumor, some investors could have already profited by shorting the stock, which had plunged temporarily. Because of the Web, the rumor was spread easily, even though it was denied. When it comes to rumors, digital technology can be both a threat and a way of dealing with the problem.

This chapter provides strategic options and tactics for managing rumors. The activity is more art than science.

RUMOR PREVENTION

One approach is to prevent rumors by what's called "getting in front of the story" or "flooding the zone" with very detailed information and analysis that serve to address questions and concerns before they are raised. Veteran newsman Jim Wieghart advises organizations to distribute comprehensive information through all channels on any development, such as a product launch or the appointment of a new, environmentally concerned CEO.

Flooding the zone could include the traditional press release, links on the organization website, media conferences, conference calls with analysts, 24/7 hotlines, and bookings on relevant talk shows. It might also involve soliciting third-party support, such as getting the safety council of a trade association to endorse a product. Often, communications have to be custom-made for each constituency, be it government regulators, shareholders, or supply chain vendors.

In this time of upheaval in the workplace, and with the passage of laws such as the Lilly Ledbetter Fair Pay Act and other employee-rights legislation, business organizations usually flood the zone with information in the wake of layoffs, revision of benefits, or outsourcing of jobs overseas. That limits the space in which rumors can start and gain traction. Lack of information and perceived evasiveness are breeding grounds for rumor.

RUMOR REARS ITS HEAD

Rumor is inevitable in a time of so much change and so many channels of communication. That's why organizations now use a variety of services, ranging from Technorati to sites such as UrbanLegendsOnline.com, to monitor print, digital, audio, and video communications. Companies are on the lookout for information, misinformation, malice, emotion, or whatever else could lead to, or involve, rumors about them. The scope of the monitoring depends on the organization.

In politics, monitoring is often comprehensive. In fact, many political organizations, especially during campaigns, have a dedicated control center—even a war room—for picking up on what is being said, making decisions on how to deal with it, and implementing those decisions.

In a business, it's less so, unless the company is at the center of a very significant event such as a major product launch, scandal, or reduction in force. Ordinarily, companies monitor key media covering their industry, competition, and government.

Each rumor is an entity unto itself. There are many scenarios for how a rumor came to be, and why, and the most efficient and effective way to cope with it. For example:

1. *The rumor may be a plus for the organization.* It might be speculation in chat rooms and bulletin boards that the company will sponsor a contest seeking user-created content for its Super Bowl commercial. Given that the idea is already out there, the company might decide to release an announcement addressing the matter earlier than planned. Or perhaps the company leaked the information to catalyze interest and enhance its reputation. In this case, leverage the attention.

2. *The speculation may not be worth paying attention to, and might simply vanish if ignored.* An example may be the rumor that a popular brand of cereal might be preparing to make a major change in its ingredients. Addressing the rumor can give it a life of its own.

3. *Rumors that can potentially damage an organization have to be addressed.* Therefore, as part of the overall crisis plan, there should also be a plan in place for how to respond to such rumors. In this scenario:

   - The response plan should specify who the spokesperson will be, what the approval procedures are for relevant functions such as legal and manufacturing, and how and when information should be released. The distribution systems for the initial response and the ongoing follow-up should also be decided beforehand, including key media to notify and posting on the organization's website.
   - The response plan must include the message to be communicated. For instance, if the rumor relates to contamination during food processing, the message might be that since 1987, systems have been in place, and they are constantly inspected and continually updated to prevent contamination.
   - Control over the message and therefore over the situation comes from gathering and releasing the facts as quickly and completely as they become available. When they are not available, spokespeople can indicate they will report the facts as soon as possible. Rumors can catch organizations by surprise. Suppose there is speculation that the CEO is about to be fired. A response is expected

to be rapid, especially when material information is involved. Security analysts and shareholders need to know the facts.

- In preparing a response, there will always be the push and pull between the lawyers and the spokespeople. Usually, a compromise can be worked out. The lawyers can protect the organization while the public statements communicated express a human sensibility. Gone are the days when legal concerns were excuses for stonewalling or saying "No comment." If the organization is wrong, the lawyers and the communications folks can create a mea culpa that puts the best possible face on the situation in order to prevent litigation yet satisfy the constituencies. Organizational rhetoric is expected to be conversational.
- Symbolism is powerful, particularly when it involves action. Consider a rumor that senior executives are receiving big bonuses as a firm is laying off 23 percent of its workforce. The response cannot be just a denial of the rumor; it should include the announcement, for example, that the top 100 executives are taking a 10 percent reduction in pay.
- Third-party support can provide unique credibility. Often, it's what others say about an organization that can carry more weight than what an organization says about itself. Take the rumor that the company discriminates on the basis of gender. Professional organizations whose mission is women's equality in the workplace can go on record supporting the company's record in hiring, developing, compensating, and promoting females.
- If it becomes necessary to turn over the investigation of facts to an independent agency, make sure that outside organization has a credible reputation.
- If necessary, switch the channel. This is an era of short attention spans. What is of interest this afternoon might not be on the digital radar screen come the evening. This process can be ensured by introducing a new subject. For instance, information about a possible new product line is rumored. Counter with an announcement about restructuring the design department.

PERSISTENT RUMORS

Of course, some rumors just won't die, at least not easily. One enduring example is the alleged satanic symbolism associated with Procter & Gamble. That urban legend has had a too-long shelf life. Others are that President John F. Kennedy is alive but disabled in a nursing facility; that his late son was not really his son; and that Enron CEO Ken Lay faked his death.

Jim Wieghart has studied this matter. His conclusion: "When rumors persist, we have to ask, 'What do the people behind those rumors really want?'" Wieghart recommends digging to discover real motives.

- *Is there a question that hasn't been raised that is therefore not answered?* That's the elephant in the room issue. To illustrate, a rumor is swirling around the organization that the CEO had an affair with an intern. One of the questions on people's minds, but never articulated, is whether his spouse, a partner in a law firm, was ever home. People want to know, but don't even realize that they do. The answer turned out to be yes. The wife was known to play hostess at various social events at the CEO's home.
- *Do those pushing the rumors want something concrete, such as jobs, a membership on the board of directors, or a financial settlement?* If so, then a decision has to be made whether to negotiate on these demands.
- *Could the escalating rumors be leading up to a threatened lawsuit?* In this litigation-sophisticated era, excessive public attention to a possible, or actual, lawsuit could encourage a generous confidential payout. Organizations have to determine if complying will simply generate more lawsuits.
- *Is the rumormongering intended to establish a media presence?* That's a standard tactic for muckrakers. In this case, the best response might be no response. It takes two to feed the momentum of a rumor.

EMERGING MORE THAN WHOLE

The art of managing rumors can result in emerging from the ordeal more than whole. A classic case is the manner in which Hillary Clinton gained sympathy and support during a time of constant speculation about the state of her marriage. She remained calm. In public, she played the role of the dedicated spouse and her husband did the same. Dignity was the name of the game.

To increase the odds that a rumor can be turned into an opportunity, some guidelines are helpful:

- Never react. That provides fuel for the opposition.
- Craft one responsive message and keep reinforcing it. Being a "broken record" discourages the agitators.
- Express compassion for the attackers. That defuses their power. After all, they must be needy souls to have to engage in this mischief.
- Have everyone in the loop stick together.
- Share with constituencies how much one is learning from the situation. It's all about lessons learned.

TAKEAWAYS

- Rumor plays many roles in a society. The more volatile or ambiguous a situation, the more rumors there will be, and they are bound to strengthen.
- Rumors take a variety of forms. They include a fevered search for information, investigative journalism relying on sources, leaks to test out an idea, attempts to damage an opponent, and intentions to manipulate information for gain—usually, financial.
- Rumors can often be prevented by what's called "getting in front of the story" or "flooding the zone" with information. That entails pulling out all stops by making detailed

information and analysis available for all constituencies and anticipating concerns; it could involve the use of questions and answers, hotlines, and just-in-time media conferences. Embedded in all this should be the overall message about the product, department, or leadership involved.

- Most rumors demand no response. Don't feed the momentum and it may deflate.
- Organizations must have a plan in place for monitoring and dealing with rumors. It could be part of the overall crisis plan. It must include a message that favorably positions the target of the particular rumor.
- Rumors tend to persist because those keeping them alive haven't gotten what they want. Sometimes they don't actually know what their goal really is and the organization has to ferret it out.
- Managed artfully, rumors can enhance one's positioning.

CHAPTER

CRISIS COMMUNICATIONS

"Everything in crisis communications sends a message, intentionally or not."

—Bill Armstrong

THERE'S NOTHING NECESSARILY SCARY about a crisis. A crisis is simply an urgent development that demands the right kind of communications. In itself it might not be real. It could even be someone else's crisis, which provides another organization with an edge if it positions and packages the opportunity just right.

Among the many forms of crisis, the lion's share falls into three categories.

One occurs whenever the now-24/7, increasingly digital media decide a crisis is taking place. That designation could apply equally to a global financial meltdown or to lower SAT scores in Greenwich, Connecticut. In short, it's not necessarily about what happened or didn't happen. It is about rolling out negative news. And what's negative has a selling advantage. Any organization can get caught in this cycle.

The second kind of crisis is an event or unfolding saga that reasonable people agree is a threat or has already caused serious harm. As the world economy, supply chains, laws, political alliances, and climate issues become more interrelated, this type of crisis is becoming the new normal. The points of intersection among everything from financial markets to jet travel exponentially increase the number and severity of these crises.

The third variety is someone else's crisis, and if an organization acts quickly and appropriately, it can be turned into gold. Remember the lead hazards associated with toys imported from China? Hasbro, which didn't have Chinese suppliers, leveraged that situation as a marketing tool during the Christmas season. Since, for so many organizations, crisis is inevitable, learning how to channel it into opportunity for one's own enterprise is a "must-do."

Digital technology has not much affected how to manage a crisis. The impact of digitalization seems to be confined to creating the perception of a crisis and delivering the news in diverse formats, ranging from aggregator sites to blogs to YouTube.

In fact, how public relations professionals approach crisis communications hasn't changed significantly from the early 1980s. That's when the gains Johnson & Johnson derived from its masterful handling of Tylenol tampering became obvious. After that, the best and brightest in communications formed a consensus on what strategies and tactics help organizations exit crises intact or even emerge, as did J&J, in better shape than when they entered.

FUNDAMENTALS

This chapter spells out the fundamentals of communicating during crisis. The goal is to preserve the organization's assets, ranging from product marketability and stock price to brand name. The way of achieving that goal is through control of the message. Bill Armstrong, a principal with The Dilenschneider Group, stresses that all crises send a message, intentionally or otherwise. Accordingly, it is far better for the organization to control that message than allow it to be controlled by other parties.

In that regard, crisis communications is no different from other areas of public relations. Similarly, too, when dealing with crisis, there will be multiple constituencies. Those constituencies might include the organization, law enforcement, people directly affected such as families of the dead or injured, medical facilities, the media, shareholders, supply chain members, communities, and third-party allies, including the clergy.

Of course, each crisis is unique. No two are identical, especially in the emotional experience and memory bank of those who endure them. However, there are proven guidelines that apply to all crisis situations.

TRUSTED INSIDER

Crisis communications begins with choosing the public relations "pro" who can, and will, have the trust of the organization's head. The pro has to be able to be the ultimate insider. That leader must also have the self-confidence and sense of responsibility to push back on the organization, over and over again. Those push-backs might entail going to the mat to label a situation a risk, ensuring accurate facts are disclosed, or mobilizing the organization to seize the potential in someone else's bad fortune. This kind of pro is a sort of seer. Armstrong describes the pro as someone who "must be omniscient about risk." Crisis occurs when risk becomes a negative reality.

The pro has to make the judgment calls about what the risks are for an organization. To do that, the pro must have as much access to operations and information as the head of the organization does. Anything less leaves the organization exposed to negatives and closed to the positive impacts.

RISK ASSESSMENT

Assessing risk, at the very least, calls for determining:

- What could go wrong? A global supply chain might contain vulnerabilities involving food safety, sweatshop labor conditions, or domestic agitation about outsourcing.
- How likely is that to occur? What could reduce the likelihood of things going wrong?
- What are the competition's risks and what advantage could come to the organization if there was a crisis, say, in product quality? Apple seized an advantage when Microsoft released its problem-ridden Vista operating system.
- What kinds of direct negative and positive impacts could there be on people, property, international relations, revenues, lawsuits, and brand name? Any harm to people is the most serious concern. Any benefit coming to people should be leveraged.

- What are the indirect impacts, positive and negative?
- What impacts can be prevented or at least minimized?
- How should the organization address worst-case scenarios? Are the resources available, or can they be secured just-in-time?

This assessment is ongoing. It has to be. In a global economy, external conditions could cause broad consumer concern in the United States; that concern, if positioned correctly, could present new opportunities as well. The melamine-contamination epidemic originating in China is an example of a crisis that also generated more market share for food companies that use only U.S. suppliers.

THE PLAN

The public relations pro should create an overall plan for managing a crisis well before it may happen, whether it is a media-made or man-made negative event. That plan, counsels Armstrong, who has handled crises for more than twenty years, must include the following details:

- The name of the contact person in charge, plus all contact numbers and digital addresses. Having essential, accurate statistical data available is critical. For example: Joe Smith is the contact and he can be reached at (landline, cell phone, e-mail). Every function and operation has to be nailed down this way.
- The names of everyone else inside the organization who must be notified, when, in what order, and their contact information. Establishing these lines of disclosure is imperative.
- All people outside of the organization who must be notified, in what order, and their contact information. After a plant accident, for example, family members of the dead and injured have to be notified before the media.
- A designated spokesperson. Except in unusual circumstances, this spokesperson should be the public relations pro, at least initially, in order to create distance between the CEO and the

crisis. When appropriate, the CEO can be brought to the media and other constituencies, usually alongside the spokesperson. Early bad news should come from the spokesperson. For early good news, the CEO should make the announcement. The spokesperson can be the internal PR pro already on the scene or the pro from the company's hired agency.

- A mandate that facts are only released through the one spokesperson. This order prevents others internally from speculating or giving misinformation or premature data. It also allows the message to be framed within the facts. That message would, of course, vary with the nature of the crisis. It could be that the organization has always made safety first or that the organization sees quality as job number-one.

THE FACTS AS MESSAGE

When the negative event occurs, the pro is responsible for collecting as many facts as are available at the time. Only those facts, no matter how incomplete, will be released according to the order specified in the plan. Urgency always rules, but the plan has to be followed. It might be necessary to announce: "We are gathering the facts. Right now, all that we know is that an explosion happened at the Port Arthur Oil Refinery at about 10:00 a.m. We do not as yet know if there were any human injuries or the extent of the property damage."

Once the facts start coming in, they should be transmitted to all constituencies in the form of a message. Never are the facts delivered in their raw state.

That messaging extends beyond the words to the venue where the words are said. That's called "staging." Ideally, the spokesperson should address the media, as well as all other constituencies, from a location that is neutral or even positive.

In the event of a destructive fire or explosion, the spokesperson should not talk in front of a burning building. The briefing could take place almost anywhere else. As another example, let's say a client is ending a jail term. Then, the spokesperson will try to arrange for the client to speak to the media in a setting away from the prison gates that best reinforces the message of moving on to a new life. Staging might also entail bringing in law enforcement, clergy, or other third parties whose presence can be reassuring to constituencies.

As the facts continue to become available, the spokesperson should schedule regular times for briefing the media. That is a way to maintain control over the press. Members of the press have to defer to the organization's time frame.

TONE

The spokesperson's tone has to be conversational. A crisis situation demands plain language and simple sentence structure. Anything more formal undercuts sincerity and empathy.

In addition, the tone always conveys great gravitas. Even if the situation is tailor-made for a late-night joke, the spokesperson retains a somber persona. For example, a shopper gets seriously bitten by a large, runaway animal a block from a store's parking lot. The store expresses compassion, even though it has no intention of assuming liability. The message is: "We are a caring organization. This wasn't a joke to the person who was injured, nor is it to us."

But, suppose the facts emerge that the organization is somehow responsible for the injury and its lawyers determine the store has liability for the incident. Here, the appropriate messaging is to disclose those facts in a way that communicates the store's caring organizational culture and its continuous improvement of all systems, including safety. In its statement, the store admits its error in judgment, assumes responsibility, and explains how it will prevent this kind of occurrence in the future. Mea culpas, when issued quickly and sincerely, can end the story—and the crisis. Human beings, fallible creatures that most are, tend to be quite forgiving.

Should lawyers be allowed onstage? Not unless litigation has already been filed. Bringing on the lawyers tends to distract from the message. Moreover, any legal statement should be translated into human-speak. Legalese sends out a red flag that the organization might be trying to conceal something through legal tricks.

UNANSWERED QUESTION

Why do some crises end fairly rapidly and others drag on? In the latter case, usually a question about the situation remains both unarticulated and unanswered. With that issue hovering, the shadow hangs over the organization or the individual.

One can cite many examples. The Ponzi scheme of investment adviser Bernard Madoff remained fixed in the global, collective consciousness. Then, forensic psychologists began to speculate about the question that turned out to be on everyone's mind: Why did he do what he did? Theories emerged. The media focus on Madoff mitigated somewhat, until his sentencing, as the public sought motives. When a crisis persists, dig for what question is not being addressed.

CREATING NEW VALUE

It's possible to exit from a negative crisis in better shape than before it occurred. The classic case is the 1982 Tylenol scare. At the time, Johnson & Johnson demonstrated integrity by making the considerable financial sacrifice of removing every single product from the shelves in mostly unaffected locales. This ended the risk and relieved consumers. For years, a positive aura surrounded Johnson & Johnson.

This approach—integrity over profits—is what plaintiff's attorney Bill Marler, partner in Marler Clark law firm, advises companies that have been sued for food-borne diseases to follow. Marler recommends that they compensate victims up front—even before litigation proceeds—for medical costs.

That's the major concern of families. Out-of-pocket expenses, insured or not, can be huge. For the uninsured, they are catastrophic. Paying those costs does not constitute admission of guilt. It is simply a goodwill gesture rendered to needy people. It could prevent the case going to trial. If there is a trial, then everyone in the loop—plaintiff, jury, or media—could be more favorably disposed to the defendant.

USE IT OR LOSE IT

When a competitor is entangled in a crisis, the door is open to exploit the message that one's own organization is strong in areas where the competitor is weak. A big pharma company is nailed for marketing drugs for off-label uses. The message from another pharma company might be that it has a record of 100 percent compliance with federal regulations. A crisis plan should include "what-if" scenarios and positive messaging that leverage the competitor's possible stumbles and scandals.

Since no two crises are alike, it is shrewd to deconstruct how other organizations handle theirs. This could turn out to be the invaluable preparation for what may be next.

TAKEAWAYS

- A crisis can be media-made, man-made, and not always negative.
- Crisis communications means controlling the message. The audience consists of multiple and often diverse constituencies.
- Controlling the message allows the organization to emerge whole or even better off.
- Risk assessment is imperative and ongoing.
- The plan for managing a crisis must detail lines of authority and disclosure of information.
- Staging is as important as words.
- Integrity is a priceless form of added value.

SECTION THREE

THE BROADER PR SPECTRUM

The public relations sector spills over into many specialized areas that require very specific and sophisticated communications skills. A number of those areas—notably, government relations, the huge tourism and travel industry, and investor relations—are dealt with in some depth in the following chapters.

CHAPTER

GOVERNMENT RELATIONS

"The presidential campaign of 2008 showed that technology can be used not only to communicate a message, but to organize people online. Those thousands of mini-organizations become message ambassadors, special-event hosts, fund-raisers, and more."

—Jim Wieghart

IN 1999, POLITICAL CONSULTANT Dick Morris predicted how the Internet would give everyman and everywoman a direct voice in electing officials, influencing legislation, and righting wrongs. In his book *Vote.com*, Morris said this development would usher in the era of "direct democracy" that Thomas Jefferson envisioned.

The presidential campaign of 2008 proved Morris right, but also that he wasn't bold enough in his prediction. Candidate Barack Obama's strategists showed that technology has an extraordinary ability to organize people online, as noted by veteran journalist Jim Wieghart, former editor of the *New York Daily News*.

This chapter explores how all constituencies, ranging from government representatives to corporations to outraged Main Street, can influence and likely change the status quo, going well beyond straightforward lobbying. That status quo might be policies that fail to protect human rights, impede sales, and make the stock market seem rigged. Had Martin Luther King Jr. been alive in the Internet age, he probably would be making fewer in-person addresses and focusing more on organizing activists and raising funds online.

GOVERNMENT RELATIONS

In essence, what is called "government relations" is a form of power. In his historic 1990 book *The Power Game*, Washington, D.C., journalist Hedrick Smith explained that there are myriad types of power. There is the power of position, as in having the title of U.S. Senator or U.S. President. There are other types of power, too, that come from having access, confidence, imagination, an ability to create obstacles, and media savvy.

The power of those engaged in government relations is the proven ability to affect outcomes. A candidate is elected. A bill is passed or not passed. A congressional investigation does or does not take place. A new cabinet post is or is not created. A nominee for the U.S. Supreme Court is confirmed or not. Those with this power earn great respect and often lucrative incomes. It is one of the most valued abilities in the twenty-first century.

That wasn't always the situation, of course. In more idealistic times, such as the stable, prosperous post–World War II period, this power of influence was often vilified. Those engaged in it were known as "influence peddlers." Even today, the names of some influence peddlers, such as Jack Abramoff, carry with them the stench of corruption and a system that's tilted toward those with wealth. Admittedly, not everyone with the power of influence is a good guy. Like all forms of power, this one is open to abuse.

However, the Internet has helped end that naïve understanding about how things get done, including in politics. Lone blogger Matt Drudge broke open the sex scandal involving a sitting president and an intern. The rest is political history. There are a growing number of online communities focused on influencing policies—local, regional, national, and global. They range from activists to businesses. Even the relatively conservative pharmaceutical industry, report Frank Vellucci and Eddie Huang on Law.com, has been "weighing the positives and negatives of Web 2.0" for informing and organizing constituencies ranging from physicians to consumers.

Rather than being suspect, the power of government relations is recognized as a needed function in the complex global society of the twenty-first century. It operates in all directions—from and to government, among constituencies, and on the periphery experimenting with activism.

FUNDAMENTALS

No matter what tools are used—print, digital, audio, video, or in-person communications—the fundamentals for effectiveness remain the same:

- *Personal contacts always have and always will carry the Midas touch of influence.* For instance, it is useful to be known as having relationships with leaders, aides to politicians, activists, agitators, polling experts, campaign managers, political speechwriters, and digital architects.
- *Relationships can begin, be nurtured, and be strengthened through socializing.* Influence is, in many ways, a game that is made to appear as played out in the open. Yes, the public enjoys gawking. That's exactly why the digital site Gawker.com had been so popular for years. Those who have access or want it attend high-profile events, as well as intimate ones that are widely broadcast, as in "John Smith and his wife, Mona, enjoyed a quiet dinner at Senator X's home in his home district."
- *Publicity about relationships is important.* However, photo ops are less so. In fact, in this media-savvy era, they could become items of ridicule. What counts is being invited to those events, being spotted at them, and having that presence reported by word-of-mouth, word-of-mouse, and the mainstream media.
- *Relationships are enhanced through fund-raising, in all its combinations and permutations.* They could include establishing and operating a political action committee (PAC), sponsoring events to raise money, launching a digital initiative to build a candidate's war chest, lending one's celebrity or brand name to fund-raising, and contributing large amounts.
- *How the person, or the organization, is being perceived in the media and on Main Street matters.* This is an era of brutal digging for negatives about individuals and groups. That means leadership and the organizational track record have to be carefully vetted. The next step is determining the advantages and disadvantages of attributes stemming from the leader's identity, such as being gay, divorced, or a recovered substance abuser, and then leveraging the advantages to outweigh the disadvantages. Congressman Barney Frank's team seems to have done an excellent job of that. Perception, of course, can change with the times.

- *Those with influence got there because they were and are adept at playing the political game.* Therefore, it's imperative to figure out what will persuade them. Will it be an offer to help in the next election, or support for a pet project? Arguing the pure worth of an issue is just a part, and often a small part, of an approach to those in the position to make decisions. Success is most likely to come when the pitch is made gracefully, but with laserlike precision. Study the leader's current positioning, strengths and vulnerabilities, mission, vision, goals, and voting track record.
- *It is beneficial, obviously, to understand the issue, but from the points of view of those with influence or the major stakeholders.* One's own perception may not be relevant. What is relevant is to position and package it so that it gets attention from the right people.
- *The skillful use of emotion trumps every other appeal.* Political psychologist Drew Westen documented that in his 2007 book, *The Political Brain.* The trick is to embed the emotion in standard arguments about the issue. Those might include scientific evidence, expert testimony, surveys, and support by other constituencies. To illustrate, in a courtroom, no matter how heinous a crime and how easy it would be for a prosecutor to lead the jurors to convict based on moral revulsion, courtroom procedure and decorum require presentation of evidence, points of law, and appeal to community values. Society demands reason to justify an emotional decision.
- *You can never do just one thing, or rely on one thing, even if it proves to be a home run.* Do everything initially and continue with multiple tactics. If the primary medium is digital, then the hackers will focus on that. Multiple tactics could include old-fashioned door-to-door lobbying, conducting town meetings, phoning, e-mailing, arranging performance art events such as flash crowds and street theater, meeting in person with the powers-that-be, blogging, podcasting, leveraging social networks such as Facebook, using snail mail, penning opinion-editorials and letters to the editor for the print media, participating in television and radio talk shows, sending

comments into those forums, setting up speaker's bureaus, obtaining celebrity and other brand-name support, distributing flyers on cars, and just being there in public spaces with a message. Focus on the top four or five tactics that work best. Then, have them reinforce each other. Influence is an interrelated system. Outcomes are produced from all those parts interacting together.

- *You must measure outcomes.* Enthusiasm can exaggerate the impact of any tactic, so keep measuring. In issue management, factors can change abruptly. Monitoring results can help strategists pick up on those shifts immediately.
- *Repetition is what cements a point of view.* Therefore, be persistent. You must make sure the need for action is drilled into the consciousness of those who matter. This is particularly the case in this era of limited attention spans.
- *Published books are a means of getting attention on a topic.* Notice how many of the players in Campaign '08 had books out there. Books, even if they aren't read, provide an aura of legitimacy and credibility.

THE MESSAGE

Some messages resonate and some don't. Some increase support and some kill it. Some endure and some fade even before an audience leaves a town meeting. What goes into crafting the message that will effectively communicate the point of view with the right constituencies, at the right time? Here are some knowns:

- *The message should mirror or reflect the mind-set and feelings of those you want to persuade.* Every successful salesperson knows that. Human beings are receptive and responsive to what aligns with what's inside of them. Actually, there is now scientific evidence for this. It's called "mirror neurons." Italian researchers, including neuroscientist Marco Iacoboni, uncovered the reason no man is an island. In 2008, Iacoboni wrote a much-praised book on the subject, *Mirroring*

People: The New Science of How We Connect with Others. The pitfall here is mirroring in inept ways that put other people on guard. They perceive the "other" as an outsider, an intruder, a manipulator. Some of presidential candidate Hillary Clinton's mirroring tactics may have fallen into the category of inept. Much more skillful was former President Bill Clinton's "I feel your pain."

- *Positive, in the long run, trumps negative.* The so-called Great Communicator, Ronald Reagan, intuitively recognized this fact. That is probably why he always avoided being the messenger bearing bad news and engaging in confrontation. In Campaign '08, the Democratic candidates' messages were more positive than those of their Republican opponents, however. Or perhaps it just came off that way. At the beginning of his first 100 days in office, when President Barack Obama's message was perceived as dark, he might have been advised to lighten up. His message did, in fact, soon become full of optimism and hope.
- *In the short run, though, negative can be effective.* Communications based on fear and hate might, initially, gain critical mass. That is how famous populists such as Huey Long obtained power. However, attack politics will not work for an extended outreach. Because negative messages consume a great deal of energy to digest, the audience tires and may turn on the leader.
- *From the overall message, subthemes should be custom-made for individual segments.* This is the era of diverse values and lifestyles. Members of large groups rarely are homogeneous or represent a monolith. It's often "message suicide" to target exclusively "the Midwest," "the Over-55 Crowd," or "the Unemployed." However, the submessage has to be a perfect fit with the general message. It should be played out as the variation on a theme. Media will pick up on inconsistencies, along with the opposition.
- *The message must be simple, as brief as possible, concrete, provocative, not platitude-ridden, and rooted in human experience.* Generations of students have been taught these same lessons because that's how discourse is communicated.

Cuba's Fidel Castro became a global joke when he departed from every one of those guidelines in his three- and four-hour harangues.

- *The message must be done right the first time.* Message-change, just like brand-change, sends a red flag; is hard work; and usually isn't successful. That's why research is imperative and every tactic should be used to test out a message. (Chapter 19 of this handbook discusses research, including low-cost approaches.)

DIGITAL INITIATIVES

Case studies of the notably successful digital strategy used by candidate Barack Obama have been created for analysis in myriad disciplines, ranging from political science and public affairs to information technology and network architecture. There will be plenty more case studies as businesses increasingly employ the Web, especially to launch and grow grassroots efforts.

One of the easiest of the case studies to read was written by Ellen McGirt in the April 2009 edition of *Fast Company*. McGirt noted that the primary tool the candidate used was My .BarackObama.com, or MyBo, a user-friendly networking site. By the time the race was won, there were some 2 million profiles on the site; 35,000 groups had been formed; 200,000 events had taken place on behalf of the candidate; 400,000 posts had been made on blogs; 70,000 personal fund-raising pages were created; and countless millions of dollars were raised.

Another insightful deconstruction is made by Internet expert Don Tapscott, who approaches the Obama campaign's digital effort within the context of the net-generation, or Millennials. He devotes a chapter in *Growing Up Digital* to describing the work of the architect of that strategy, Chris Hughes. A pioneer on social network site Facebook, Hughes was able to use digital tools "to disrupt convention, topple authority, and potentially change the world." The "killer app" was to provide on the site the necessary technology for supporters to organize their own mini-campaigns. It's analogous to those advertising contests that allow entrants to download whatever they need to create their own commercials for Doritos or Chevy.

From all that has been said about both the Obama campaign strategy and using digital media, in general, in government relations, there are some lessons learned:

- *Give people ownership of a mission, vision, or cause and they will not only do the job, but go the extra mile.* All generations supported Obama online, not just the net-generation. The tone and language of a site should be all about "you," not "us" or, worse, "me."
- *Take time experimenting with the site before official launch.* It is shrewd to interview a number of vendors to pick their brains about approaches and find the right chemistry. If possible, learn from the digital experience of others. Hughes absorbed plenty from his days with Facebook.
- *Monitor what the opponent or competition is up to digitally.* Stay current with them or, much better, ahead.
- *Have permission to capture names, e-mail addresses, and user information online for a database.* This is one of the gold mines associated with a digital outreach. Analyze that data. Keep in touch with those visitors.
- *Treasure feedback, especially when it is negative.* Any feedback constitutes free consulting on a digital outreach. Discern where the praise and criticism are on the money and apply that new knowledge to the site.
- *Communicate integrity and develop trust through a real voice.* Not everyone might like every aspect of one's online persona, but at least it will come across as authentic. Be personally there and continually responsive. Sustained presence is everything. It can be accomplished through multiple sites that are linked together. On Twitter, candidate Barack Obama had 20,000 followers whom he always kept up-to-date on how he saw the campaign going, where he was traveling to next, and how he felt about developing issues and breaking news. Instinctively, human beings long for some kind of leadership.

- *Provide the tools people need for participation.* For grassroots campaigns, such as one by a pharmaceutical company to encourage Medicare recipients to lobby for certain kinds of reimbursement, provide simple-to-understand discussion of the issue, expert opinion, testimonials, interactive capability, links to other information, click-on e-mail addresses to contract government representatives, and incentives for participating. People want a sense of belonging. Membership, as the old American Express commercial touted, has its privileges.

- *Establish a reputation as a "must-check-first" site.* Since the metabolism of the Web is speedy, the rhythm of the postings must be hypomanic or, at least, just-in-time. On issues such as breaking developments and other kinds of relevant news, the site should be the first one people want to check. If it isn't, it may never be visited again. People are creatures of habit. Get them in the habit of pulling up the site several times daily.

- *Attract people by being entertaining.* People of all chronological ages love entertainment. Wit, humor, irony, parody, and satire can create added value. Comic-book characters and versions of Japanese manga fit the bill with the net-generation. Real-life renditions of these fictional characters emblazoned on paraphernalia such as shirts and banners can both reinforce the effort and raise money. Cartoons also work nicely.

- *Reinforce digital efforts in mainstream media.* The two are symbiotic. A strong digital presence should never count out developing relationships with print journalists and editors and television network producers. A blog post or e-mail campaign that brings down a server is news that mainstream media want to hear about. Tell them. This cross-media involvement is a "must-do."

- *Use database information to organize in-person special events.* Word-of-mouse will be further cemented by word-of-mouth and the personal touch.

- *Operate digital sites for instant polling and other kinds of surveys, then post the results.* Bring the numbers, and an interpretation of the findings, to the attention of mainstream media. Yes, any sampling of public opinion is perceived and treated as news.

- *Experiment—locally, nationally, and globally—with what's being called "digital brainstorms."* Essentially, these are online forums that allow people to form a virtual think tank or virtual town hall meeting. One such event was conducted by the government of Canada, using technology from IBM, in 2005, with the goal of soliciting ideas about urban sustainability. Almost 40,000 folks participated. Don Tapscott describes that innovation in *Growing Up Digital.*
- *Stay positive and constructive.* Going on the attack echoes old-line, one-way politics. One can almost smell the cigar smoke from those days.
- *Develop new kinds of digital initiatives.* That in itself will generate useful publicity for the leader, issue, or cause. In turn, more visitors will come to the site to check out what's going on. Those casual browsers could become grassroots volunteers, fund-raisers, and major contributors. People like to participate in what's judged as cool. Costs can be high, but so can the payoff.

COURSE CORRECTION

Nothing erodes that fragile entity known as trust like a mistake that isn't acknowledged and then fixed; a scandal that isn't addressed, with measures taken to prevent it in the future; and sins of omission not admitted. Course correction, immediate and thorough, is imperative. It may be necessary to wait until the facts are in, but even in those situations, someone must step up to the plate, indicate concern, and report that an investigation is under way and the facts will be reported as soon as they are available.

Most human beings, at least the mature ones, are in touch with their own myopia and their own possible worst selves. Therefore, they tend to forgive transgressions by others. What's not forgiven is the cover-up or any attempt to put a cover-up in place. Forgiveness was a standard in one-way politics until Watergate. After that, no leader who has been caught in some kind of wrongdoing has ever fully recovered. That includes former President Bill Clinton. His legacy will always carry the taint of "I did not have sex with that woman." Crises blow over. Cover-ups linger in the national and global memory bank.

TAKEAWAYS

- The successful digital strategy of Campaign '08 has changed government relations forever.
- As predicted by political consultant Dick Morris in 1999, digital technology gives everyman and everywoman a voice in government and the low-cost, high-reach, easy-to-use tools to organize on a grassroots basis. Government relations is no longer a function carried out by professionals. That in itself raises the bar for performance by those who are paid professionals.
- Some fundamentals, such as the importance of personal contacts, don't change.
- The message should be created right the first time and adapted for subgroups.
- From case studies of Campaign '08, lessons have been derived about using digital outreach in politics. The most important of those lessons might be this: It takes patience to set up and test out a site.
- Course correction must be immediate and comprehensive.

CHAPTER

TRAVEL AND TOURISM

"The U.S. is a traveling country. Americans have come to view travel as a fundamental entitlement. Although vacation travel was once considered a luxury, in today's world it has for many become a necessity—during challenging as well as robust economic times."

—Joan Brower and Joan Bloom

TRAVEL AND TOURISM, a multibillion-dollar global industry, has always relied heavily on promotion and publicity to showcase the huge number of destinations, attractions, and vacation options—hotels, resorts, regions, and countries—competing for travel business, not to mention the army of carriers, airlines, trains, cruise ships, buses, and other vehicles to transport travelers to those destinations. So vital is the industry that there are entire venues (including smaller nations) whose economies are almost wholly dependent on tourism.

TRAVEL PR IN A DIGITAL AGE

As in most other sectors, the digital revolution has had a profound impact on the travel and tourism industry—both in terms of marketing (Orbitz, Expedia, Travelocity, Priceline) and promotion (destination websites, online travel media, blogs, chat rooms/forums, YouTube, travel-based search engines, social networks, mobile media sharing, e-mail blasts). Viral is the operative word.

The impact of social media on the promotion of travel is particularly powerful and growing exponentially. In fact, word-of-mouth in the travel sphere is valued as much as traditional advertising or even editorial reporting. Social media sites ensure that everyone can be an influencer with an independent voice, practicing what is now called "citizen journalism." Everyone can send and receive recommendations and travel endorsements within a social media group that shares common interests and characteristics.

When social media tools are applied to travel/tourism public relations campaigns, messages are carried to a wider and more diverse audience. Through digital media, consumers are able to take a much more active approach to making travel decisions.

Powerful word-of-mouth decisions enabled by social media underscore the imperative of engaging in conversations with those online communities as well as traditional media, because you want to be in the game of generating critical word-of-mouth. User-generated content means that people are listening to "people like me" rather than third-party "authority" figures. Business and leisure travelers can connect to tourism opportunities directly by tapping into any number of broad social networks on the Web. They can participate in human conversations online that influence decisions (via Facebook, MySpace, Twitter). They can be influenced by tourism messages or PR campaigns as well, and by communications employing visually striking still photos or video footage (via YouTube, Flickr). Specialized search engines such as Kayak and Bing Travel also readily identify competitive products and services from a vast universe of travel and tourism websites.

Virtual space allows travelers to self-partition into like-minded groups, just as they do in reality. By speaking and understanding the language of the online culture, travel marketers and promoters can identify those areas of special interest and demographic emphasis that relate to individual tourism preferences, and advance their business interests accordingly.

In the pre-digital era, the travel PR professional primarily targeted travel writers serving major dailies, magazines, and wire services, plus the broadcast media. Today, however, as daily newspapers are disappearing across the country, the online world has become indispensable. Travel editors and writers at numerous daily newspapers have been jettisoned, replaced by wire service and syndicate reports. Many of these journalists, whose efforts once appeared in the print media, are now writing for their own online travel sites or have joined the blogosphere.

Does this mean that communicating public relations messages via the Web is more effective than through traditional print publications? The accurate response is that they are entirely different. Diverse audiences review and analyze communications mechanisms in different ways. Their perspectives are different, and there may even be a generational divide in their preferences as well. While print publications offer the commentary of objective, third-party journalists, many of the online communications channels are the opinions of typical consumers and one's own peers. Some travelers prefer editorial information that is critiqued by authorities in the field; others prefer the "man in the street" reporting of online bloggers and chat rooms. All provide different information on different terms. Readers of print publications also migrate to the online sites of those same publications that may carry identical, or supplemental, editorial content and editorial staff.

Whatever their working medium, countless journalists continue to cover and report on travel—and that means they need to be informed and educated about available tourism offerings. One standard, venerable tactic involves "press familiarization" visits and tours, where writers are invited as guests to visit a destination—either individually or in groups. A growing segment of large, prestige newspapers and magazines have barred their writers from taking such orientation trips in the interest of protecting "editorial integrity," and this trend continues.

Meanwhile, the fierce competition among destinations demands marketing and promotion approaches that are more creative and focused than ever before. At the same time, the rise of the Internet and the decline of the travel agent's influence mean consumers have greater control over the travel selection and booking process. Finding travel deals online has expanded significantly—creating an opportunity for much greater direct-to-consumer PR applications and strategies.

TRAVEL AND THE ECONOMY

The economic downturn that began in late 2007 brought the most severe marketplace upheaval in many decades—which had a devastating effect on travel and tourism, generally. Massive layoffs, weak consumer spending, and enormous stock market losses all took their toll, reflected in sharp declines in every type of recreational spending, whether for travel, entertainment, dining, shopping, attractions, or sporting events. The recession also gave rise to a number of ongoing trends in vacation patterns and habits:

- Value has become "decider number-one" in making destination selections, spawning a flood of promotional packages to offer genuine value for the vacation dollar and justify costs.

- Vacation trips are now shorter, offering lower costs in time and money.
- More and more vacationers are using the Internet to research options, make decisions, and book their own travel, now surpassing two-thirds of all travelers.
- Mobile devices are a much bigger factor in promoting vacation destinations and closing the sale.
- The vacationing U.S. population is becoming more diversified as increasing numbers of Hispanics, Asians, and African Americans move up the economic ladder.
- PR professionals are promoting an ever-broader, more specialized universe of travelers and travel destinations.
- Special events—whether sporting, musical, or theatrical—have become key factors in attracting visitors to a particular destination.
- "Rate integrity"—maintaining pricing so as not to devalue the brand—a practice once considered unassailable, now continues to weaken as popular vacation spots increasingly offer major discounts and special packages.

THE TRAVEL SPECTRUM

Joan Bloom and Joan Brower, longtime travel industry experts who currently head the Travel & Lifestyle specialty practice at The Dilenschneider Group, have defined a number of specialized options in today's expanding travel portfolio. In addition to destinations affording sightseeing, rest, and relaxation, among the many travel trends they cite are:

- "Green travel" that promises minimal impact on the natural environment and local community. A related offshoot is "geo-tourism," which emphasizes sustaining both the culture and environment of the place being visited.
- Educational and enrichment tourism, offering participation in new learning experiences and/or immersion in culture and history.

- Domestic tourism, providing the comfort of staying closer to home in familiar, English-speaking surroundings.
- Spa and wellness travel, offering simple stress and anxiety reduction.
- Volunteerism or travel underscoring humanitarian goals and social responsibility.
- Medical tourism, reflective of the growing trend to pursue substantially lower costs for major (and minor) medical procedures in foreign lands. Tours organized for this purpose often include pre- or post-procedure sightseeing.
- Multigenerational travel that offers diversified experiences for all ages and interests—"Something for Everyone" excursions.
- "Girl Getaways" and "Mancations," where small groups of women or men with common interests share a fun-filled time together as friends in a get-away-from-it-all setting.
- Destination weddings that include family and friends in ceremonies and celebrations typically held at resort-based destinations.
- Customized travel that shapes the tourism experience according to preferred lifestyle and ethnicity, and speaks personally to different segments of the population.
- Destination reputation travel, in which consumers visit locations made famous or more interesting by association with celebrities or important historical events ("the halo effect").
- Solo vacationing that allows single travelers to explore destinations comfortably and on their own.

SOME MESSAGE THEMES

To frame and disseminate the most effective messages about a given destination, travel PR specialists should have broad-ranging knowledge of, and direct experience with, whatever site they are promoting. Typical messages might be shaped by keeping certain concepts in mind:

- Traveling with family and loved ones offers opportunities to bond and reinforce emotional support systems that reflect universal human needs.
- In challenging economic times, travelers should not feel guilty about taking vacations that provide emotional and physical mechanisms for coping with the daunting situation. "Getting away from it all" is both reasonable and necessary for the mind and body to regenerate.
- Whenever possible, ease of travel to a particular destination should be emphasized.
- In addition to the special attractions of a given destination, certain practical concerns may be addressed—but always subtly and artfully. These concerns range from terrorism, personal security, theft, and illness to local laws, currency fluctuations, political disturbances, natural disasters, and potential disappointments.

TAKEAWAYS

- The digital age has dramatically transformed the marketing and promotion of travel/tourism. Destination websites, blogs, travel-related search engines, YouTube, social networks, chat rooms, and e-mail blasts have created cybersavvy travelers. Ignore these trends at your peril.
- Nonetheless, "old media" continues to be an important part of travel/tourism public relations outreach with countless journalists—most of them freelancers—still covering the beat. The format of traditional media can impart more comprehensive analysis and description of a travel destination or product.
- The Internet and the decline of travel agent influence have given consumers significantly more control over the selection and booking process, requiring much greater direct-to-consumer applications and strategies.

- The state of the economy, an especially powerful determinant in the travel/tourism industry, has sparked numerous new trends in vacation patterns, styles, preferences, and traveler profiles.
- Special interest and niche travel is booming, triggering an ever-larger menu of specialized travel options.

CHAPTER

INVESTOR RELATIONS

"The sad truth is that there are only three types of financial prognosticators: Those who don't know, those who don't know they don't know, and those who don't know but get paid big bucks to pretend they know."

—**Burton Malkiel,** *A Random Walk Down Wall Street*

AS A CONSEQUENCE OF THE great changes in the global financial markets and the businesses whose debt and equities trade on them, the investor relations (IR) function faces a challenging future. Aside from its traditional role as the strategic, executive function of management, combining the disciplines of finance, communications, and marketing, IR now faces years of rebuilding credibility, the favorite currency of the business. Even before the financial fiasco, the introduction of technology to so many aspects of IR had changed the function in ways that are both major and minor.

According to the National Investor Relations Institute (NIRI), traditionally IR's goal has been to enhance a company's credibility while positively impacting its valuation to that of the overall market, resulting in a lower cost of capital. The job of the investor relations officer (IRO) has been to achieve this goal by providing current and potential investors with an accurate portrayal of the company's performance, the experience and depth of its management team, and its long-term prospects, as well as other intangibles.

With President Obama's proposed new regulatory program still being debated as this handbook is being written, it is difficult to predict what IR will be like in the years ahead, but we see the outline of developments that seem likely to have a profound effect on investments and, therefore, IR:

- A move to create a superagency, chartered by Congress, to replace the Securities and Exchange Commission (SEC) and the Commodity Futures Trading Commission (CFTC), and a new federal insurance regulator charged with overseeing life and health insurance and property-casualty insurance companies. Like Sarbanes-Oxley, which arose out of the excesses of the 1990s, the new regulations are expected to include penalties and punitive damages. There are influential players in each of these three sectors. And yet the anger of

Americans, caused by mounting losses of portfolios, 401(k)s, and jobs, will continue to drive a call for reform.

- Coordination internationally with the European Union and other leading powers like Japan to monitor, regulate, and enforce measures to prevent “creative transactions” and offshore havens for tax code violators. Along with this coordination will come changes in accounting rules and practices designed to make it difficult for international companies to obscure unpleasant developments.
- Pressure for real transparency in reporting financial results, along with a change in the role of independent auditors and their length of service to a company.
- Demand for real-time transactions required by a regulatory agency increasingly emboldened to make examples of violators.
- A breakup of larger financial “supermarkets,” similar to the trust-busting of the early twentieth century, to prevent concentration of financial power and, thereby, avoid having a financial crash cause the collapse of entire nations.
- Greater empowerment for boards of directors of public companies. Boards will have teeth regarding executive compensation, stock options, and the role of the nonexecutive chairman, giving that outside executive much more power to make speedy changes with the agreement of the board.

Although the financial markets and their regulations will change in some of these ways, and in others that we cannot foresee, IR will continue to be a discipline in the modern corporation with tremendous opportunities for the qualified IRO.

What lies ahead for the job and a career in IR? There will be at least two important changes in the field.

The first area is the impact of technology, which influences practically every aspect of the financial markets, investments, and IR. Technology can either be the IRO’s genie in the lamp, or it can make life more complicated than it need be. Technology should improve communications between individuals, enabling analysts to better understand the markets and fine-tune programming through technology-enabled "targeting" and through the use of IR office platforms provided by various vendors. The second area is the investment brand as a crucial development in the IR field. In the past, IROs have been counseled to "tell the investment story" or to describe the strengths of the company and its management and how its particular franchise makes for a good investment for existing and potential investors.

IMPACT OF TECHNOLOGY

Conference calls, webcasts, and websites have already changed the IRO's job. Vendors flood IROs with offers for webcasting, Internet monitoring, website integration, annual report conversions, technology platforms, and targeting. One of the most fascinating aspects of the NIRI's annual conference each June is the Investor Relations Services Showcase, where hundreds of vendors set up booths to demonstrate the latest "Star Wars" products that promise to do everything but the IRO's job.

However, the prices for these products are steep. Many of the services offered are, indeed, very useful, and some are indispensable. It is up to each IRO to determine the level of "best practices" to achieve and how much he or she can afford to spend.

Let's look at several important areas where technology can be quite useful. Remember, first, that technology is not an end in itself. Rather, technology must deliver on the objectives of the IR program. Make sure that you spell out what you want to accomplish in your plan and how each tool can help you deliver the results.

Conference Calls and Webcasts

Conference calls have always been a valuable way for companies to provide investors and the news media with a synchronized discussion of critical aspects of the earnings release and the financial results for each quarter. Company management usually won't read the news release about earnings, which can be tedious, although a few executives still do (assuming their audience has not read the release). For that reason it is better for IR to highlight important developments for management and place them in context with background. If there are major problems or questions, management can then focus on the discussion of how the financial results might be improved in the quarters ahead.

Practically every corporation today provides some sort of conference call or webcast. What's the difference? Conference calls require a telephone number, typically toll free, with the CEO, CFO, and IRO discussing the strategic overview of the company and the financial results, and with an open question period at the end. The telephone call lasts about sixty minutes, with fifteen to twenty minutes for each executive's presentation and the remaining time for Q&A, principally from the firm's sell-side analysts. The earnings release gives the 800-number and the time of the call. Conference calls are often ranked as the second or third most important source of information from a company's management. Private meetings with the CEO and CFO are usually first.

Webcasts take the audio feature of a telephone call and enable an Internet-based click-to feature that may include slides coordinated for the viewer with an explanation in the presentation. (Many companies combine both the telephone call and the webcast.) You still have to be on the phone to ask a question. So, typically, analysts and institutional investors get the 800-number and everyone else gets the Internet address from the corporate web page.

General Electric Company is a leader in various areas of IR and features its webcasts at www.ge.com. You can see immediately how to get on the webcast if you go to GE's website. The company, in short, makes it easy for you to use its IR services.

Webcasts are widespread because they tend to be faster and less expensive than conference calls. Anyone can listen anywhere with a computer. Like telephone calls, webcasts can be archived and played at a later time. It seems inevitable that more and more companies will offer real-time webcasts—much as they do now with annual shareholders meetings—so viewers can see the executives' presentations as well as hear them. Analysts and investors, who often have many calls to listen to, can write their reports and take notes while they listen to the audio. Many listeners appreciate the charts and explanatory material provided with slides that offer a visual framework for the presentation.

Websites

Most corporations today avail themselves of first-rate website developers to enhance their relationships with contacts on the Internet. If you are responsible for updates to the website, you want to make it easy for your investors to find out the latest information about shares, earnings announcements, and other developments. "Best practices" demand that you have a box or headline or button on the home page for anyone who wants to join a webcast or obtain an earnings release or an SEC document. IR's job is to make it easy for the investor.

Leading consumer brand companies like Coca-Cola, McDonald's, and AT&T have websites that cater strongly to the customer. The first thing an IR officer has to ask is how easy it is for the shareholder or institutional investor to find an IR button or contact point. Try this exercise yourself with stock you own and see how easily you can find the company's IR department online. A second concern is how easily you can find the right person to contact personally. Many more companies have begun listing the name of the IR professional and an alternative person who can be contacted directly for typical questions. Others simply have a general contact number.

The huge blogosphere is another new media space that IR professionals should be aware of. At least eighty-one Fortune 500 companies now sponsor public blogs, including Wal-Mart, Chevron, and GM, with many of the blogs linking to corporate Twitter accounts. Those blogs must walk a fine line, adhering to strict SEC rules and regulations about corporate communications without losing credibility with online audiences that expect blog postings to be outspoken and unsanitized.

Investor Relations Platforms

Technology packages designed to provide a "total picture" for the IRO are termed *platforms.* Using an IR platform is like being on the deck of the *Starship Enterprise.* The Thomson ONE platform offered by the dominant provider Thomson Reuters, for instance, is designed to provide an IRO with news about the company's shares and those of its peers in an industry, as well as other financial news feeds from Reuters. First Call service is integrated into the system so that IROs can see the latest analyst reports and the contact information for analysts who follow their companies or with whom they would like to develop a relationship. In addition, a contact database of many financial institutions in the United States and overseas allows the IR function to keep track of all meetings and contacts and to design distribution lists for news releases. Each listing contains contact information with details on holdings and investment style. The platform is thus a tool for researching the company's current shareholders and, if there is a targeting feature (as discussed in the next section), for developing lists of contacts that are likely to invest in the company.

Other features are abundant in the platforms offered by the leading vendors, probably too many for the average IRO. It's almost like using a modern smartphone or BlackBerry, where customers tend to use only a small portion of the services available. The annual subscription rates for these services vary, but they are generally in the five-figure range. There may be discounts for multiple users, but even these are probably modest when compared to the total cost.

Targeting

Targeting is essentially a lead-generation system for potential investors, similar to what a salesman would use to develop contacts for a sales call. Targeting uses computer-based criteria to evaluate a company's investment characteristics. It then takes all of the investment firms in the country and uses another set of criteria to evaluate what type of investment style the investment manager uses. Think Morningstar's Five-Star System.

None of these targeting systems is perfect. Some can be quite expensive, but they offer impressive gee-whiz features that are bound to impress most casual viewers. Potential problems with targeting include:

- Determining the metrics that best establish your company as an investment. Be sure you understand, and agree with, the developer's proposition. You may not.
- Finding out which companies you are being compared with for targeting purposes. Some targeters offer "peers." Industry peers, for a variety of obvious reasons, are useless. Investment peers may be another story. But the issue with investment peers is the comparability of your company and others.
- Understanding how the developer "targets" potential investors for you. This feature calls for the vendor to analyze all of the investment firms and give each of them a series of category designations such as "growth," "small cap," "momentum," "growth at a reasonable price" (GARP), and various other subcategories of investment style. The systems for doing this are varied and complex. Pursue the logic of the investment style. People at the investment houses do not always play fair with targeters who ask these questions. Additionally, the question is not that easy to answer. Yesterday's growth investor may be today's GARP investor.

John Lewis at Valuation Technologies (www.valtechs.com) in San Francisco has a surprisingly affordable and mathematically elegant targeting system. What is particularly appealing about VT is that it offers IROs a numerical system to see how appealing their company is as an investment to the various investment firms based on seventeen investment criteria. Like other targeting firms, VT offers detail sheets on each firm and the contact information for individuals at those firms.

This chapter only surveys the technology capabilities available to IROs today. As noted earlier, you must be the master of the servant; that is, as IRO you must integrate the technology so that it productively serves you, your management, and your board.

THE INVESTMENT BRAND

IR has morphed into a type of marketing communications. The goal is not to sell products or services per se, but to communicate what Robert E. Swadosh, an IR specialist at The Dilenschneider Group, calls the "investment brand." The IRO still retains responsibility for day-to-day tasks of collecting and filing information, plus monitoring at a minimum:

- A company's trading volume
- The entities doing the buying and selling, and the number of shares involved
- Which sell-side analysts are recommending "Buy" or "Hold," and what the details are
- Media coverage, including digital bulletin boards, chat rooms, blogs and tweets, establishment print and digital sites (such as those operated by Thomson Reuters, Bloomberg, Dow Jones, Yahoo! Finance, Google Finance, CNN Money, CNBC), and several proprietary newsletters
- Competitive intelligence of peers, both in a specific industry and in the investment sectors, which can be quite different

Game-Changers in Investor Relations

The tasks of collecting, filing, and monitoring information are only routine, not value-added. What makes the IR role a source of wealth creation and wealth growth in the twenty-first century is branding ability. Think how Apple seamlessly weaves its investment branding with the image of its organizational culture and the reputation of its products. Increasingly, the IRO pulls it all together. Perhaps more important, the IRO places certain developments in context and explains the implications to management and the board of directors. Here are two examples:

- The volatile aspects of the global economy, including fluctuating commodity prices, the erratic operations of financial markets, and the emergence of new players such as China and India, all are factors that reduce predictability. Today, the most conservative corporate leaders concede the inability to forecast the future, even within a framework of only three or six months. What is true today is not necessarily true tomorrow. The past is no longer prologue. Consequently, global corporations are eliminating quarterly earnings guidance. Instead, they are releasing just-in-time forms of information and announcements, in diverse media, in order to provide a feel for where they are at as compared with their competitors.

- Regulations put in place and litigation pursued, post-Enron, are continuing to grow in number and comprehensiveness. The factors here include the 2008–2009 Wall Street frauds, the collapse of investor confidence in equities, and a tsunami of institutional and individual losses. Sarbanes-Oxley is being strengthened, and it is just the tip of the regulatory iceberg. Anticipate a flood of class-action suits, ranging from global warming to employee rights.

Integrated Messaging

The investment brand operates much like traditional branding did back in the early 1930s. In *Brand Leadership*, David Aaker writes that at that time, the powers-that-be at Procter & Gamble noticed that the marketing of Camay soap was diffuse and uncoordinated. To fix that, a systems approach was created. All marketing decisions, from pricing to advertising, had to be made in a coordinated way; that is, with reference to the brand-management strategy. In that system, the image—which became synonymous with "brand"—was only a tactic. What counted was the integration of all elements in brand management. The result was effectiveness of marketing along with cost-efficiency.

Likewise, what could be evolving in corporations is a systemizing of messaging under Brand IR. That means all functions will be on the same page, at least in terms of the message. Years ago, Ford achieved that with the message: Quality is job one. Again, this is more than image or theme. This is what the company is about and why anyone might invest in the stock.

The framing of the brand message is increasingly taking place as an integral part of putting together the annual report. Recall the days when the annual report was produced as an expensive print glossy that provided investors, analysts, and trade media with what they probably did not know before. That hasn't been the role of the annual report for a long time now in this digital era. As digital communications have become mainstream, the annual report has evolved into a multipurpose tool for the entire corporation. (More on that subject is discussed in chapter 14.) Here, the focus is the annual report's role as a strategic platform. In some corporations, it represents the strategic brainstorming process for all functions. Everyone goes to the mat to decide what the company is and how that image is to be captured in a message format. What comes out of that process serves as the branding bible for those twelve months. Most of the concepts and language that will be part of the company's communications effort emerge from the annual report.

Rolling Out/Controlling the Message

How that overarching brand message is communicated externally and internally is wide open, as are all of the possibilities the company can and must control.

Control usually starts with the company's website. The process can begin with studying what competitors are doing with theirs. If those competitors want to stay in business, their sites will be devoid of corporatese, invite feedback, be transparent, and be updated—often daily.

Information from the company has become more critical than ever as more companies have stopped issuing quarterly earnings guidance. Among those nonissuers are Travelers, Coca-Cola, Best Buy, and Palm. Analysts, investors, and media might now expect companies to disclose via digital communications vehicles—websites, web seminars, podcasts, or YouTube—significantly more information about their portfolio of businesses.

The danger here is obvious. This sharing of information could reach the point that competitiveness can be compromised. However, the trade-off would be losing the attention of analysts, investors, the media, and other influentials. The new art is how much information to release without giving away too much. Companies adept at that could become the winners in a post-guidance IR world.

BEING INTERESTING

There are many distribution channels for making nontraditional guidance and other information available. What matters is that the format and content have to be interesting, the wording has to be in "people-speak" (i.e., avoiding corporate default terms, such as calling bad news "challenging"), and the tone must be candid.

Incidentally, what undercuts any shot at connecting with constituencies in a credible manner is overmassaging content. Too many press releases bear the marks of so much massaging that even a major law firm would be sheepish about releasing such controlled material.

Compelling, conversational, and candid are "have-tos," at least in digital times. Remember how it used to be, when a "near-nothing" event or dry development, such as a minor product upgrade, only had be turned into something resembling news when you were pitching the story to mainstream media? Now that's everyone's job. And it is hardly easy.

Currently, whatever isn't inventively positioned and packaged will be tossed, both by internal constituencies such as employees and suppliers and by external ones such as financial markets and trade media. Geico ate its competitors' lunch, dinner, and breakfast because of its fictional characters and humor, including the self-deprecating kind. An intended consequence is to have the brand identity also resonate inside the company, since employees are frequently influential brand ambassadors. Apple has created a cult, which makes all its messaging iconic. Even the Pope of the Roman Catholic Church found it smart to reach out through YouTube.

BEING THE "GO-TO" SOURCE

The objective here is simple—and represents survival. The company's own information vehicles have to become the "go-to" source for *everything*. There always were and always will be speculation, rumors, gossip, and premeditated malice. The company cannot control that. What it can control is the acceptability of its own sources as the points of clarification or confirmation.

The tone for that? It can range from serious to ironic to witty to scientific. The content? It must be accurate and complete. Openness? On everything. Be it a website, podcast, YouTube video, or blog, there must be mechanisms for easy interactivity. Blogs, in particular, operate on steroids when those putting in their two cents start chatting among themselves.

In summary, IR must contribute meaningfully to a company's overarching corporate identity, its investment brand—which is what investors evaluate every day as they consider buy and sell decisions.

Research demonstrates that 5 percent to 20 percent of a company's valuation is attributable to the strength of its corporate brand. By communicating powerful brand messages to its key constituencies, a company can enhance its reputation and build credibility at an accelerated rate. In doing so, it will also more accurately position itself to compete for mind share, market share, and capital in a rapidly changing economy.

The emerging reality of the capital markets also requires that boards and C-suites have answers to the following:

- *Vision.* What is our vision for the company's future? How aspirational is it? How attainable is it? Is the company already moving in the right direction?
- *Investment brand.* What are the key attributes of the company's investment brand? Which of these attributes support or enhance the company's underlying business model? Which of them inhibit the model?
- *Company changes.* What new brand attributes will best support or enhance requisite business model changes? Where will the current and emerging brands overlap?

Where are they inconsistent? Can any of the legacy brand attributes be updated to support the changing business model?

- *Differentiation and salience.* How differentiated is today's brand? What do we "own" today? What will we own as we are moving forward? How important is our brand to customers today? How can it be made more important?
- *Brand personality.* What is the company's brand personality? How consistent is it with our business model? With our corporate culture? How must it change?
- *Brand communications.* How is the company currently supporting (or inhibiting) its positioning with the financial community? What are its investment messages? How clear, credible, and compelling are they? How are they evolving as the business changes? What is the optimal mix of messages (strategic vs. executional) to stimulate investor interest?

TAKEAWAYS

- Articulate a clear corporate value proposition.
- Create core messages that can be utilized throughout all of the company's external and internal communications.
- Prepare to respond to macroeconomic factors that are radically changing and will continue to change IR and the role and job of the IRO.
- Make the IR mission to establish and execute the brand message.
- Know that companies can and must control the message.
- Follow the Three Cs for communications: compelling, conversational, candid.
- Deconstruct what the competition and breakthrough organizations are doing. Do better than that. Keep doing better than that.

CHAPTER

THE ANNUAL REPORT

"The annual report should take care of these investor questions: If I own the stock, should I keep it, and if I don't own the stock should I buy it?"

—JOSEPH KOPEC

THE ANNUAL REPORT (AR) HAS BEEN around for a long time. And it's not going away, at least not anytime soon. Most likely, for the foreseeable future, it will simply continue to change, perhaps significantly in the next several years.

Those changes will primarily result from the intersection of three factors: 1) what investors want to know, 2) compliance laws, and 3) technology. The pace of those changes might speed up due to the collapse of trust in the global financial system in 2008–2009. The scope could mirror those changes that took place in the early 1930s, when there was a similar erosion of investor confidence. Eventually, the impact of all that collective change could end most traditions in financial reporting, including the annual, as well as the quarterly, report.

THE OLD TRANSPARENCY

The birth of the AR, at least as a legal document, came in 1933 with the Securities Act. Supporters of that legislation, including President Franklin Roosevelt and soon-to-be U.S. Supreme Court Justice Louis Brandeis, assumed that investment in the stock market could and would be restored by transparency. Present the data and investors would have the information to make rational purchasing decisions. The excesses of the late 1920s were perceived as being generated by irrationality.

Increasingly, that assumption has come under attack. Yes, there's plenty of data out there in the 10-Ks that the Securities and Exchange Commission (SEC) requires public companies to file. These forms are made available to everyone through the SEC's EDGAR database. But that data, so plentiful and public, is presented as it relates to only one company. That is, each company computes and reports its data in idiosyncratic ways. This is all legal and is standard procedure, but it means no apples-to-apples comparisons are possible among several or all companies. And the result often is, warns investment relations expert Joseph Kopec, that the AR cannot provide answers to investors on these two key questions:

1. If I own this stock, should I keep it?
2. If I don't own this stock, should I buy it?

Kopec, who is a senior adviser to The Dilenschneider Group specializing in IR, is not alone in this concern. The National Investor Relations Institute (NIRI) agrees, as do a growing number of financial markets reformers such as Philip Moyer, CEO of EDGAR Online, Inc. As a result of this inability to gain insight about the financial position of a company via standardized comparisons with the data of other companies, often problems don't pop out as red flags, at least not soon enough.

Here's a classic example. In the April 22, 2008, edition of *Newsweek*, journalist Daniel Gross featured Merrill Lynch's AR. It was part of an article arguing that ARs are "a waste of time." At the time, the company's AR raised no great concern about the financial health of Merrill Lynch. Not long afterward, the company was in such dire financial shape that it had to be taken over. Could a standardized format for computing the numbers and presenting them have tipped off investors to Merrill Lynch's weaknesses? That question will echo through the history of financial markets in the early twenty-first century.

PROPOSED NEW TRANSPARENCY

Because so many problems remained masked and companies seemingly imploded overnight, the outcry for change in financial reporting has been escalating. The demand is for the kind of transparency in which all the numbers carry the same meaning or are standardized. In addition, it's been recommended that those numbers should go beyond the typical ones on the balance sheets and income statements. And all this data should be rolled out in a simplified format.

The payoff, reports Daniel Roth in *Wired*'s March 2009 article on fixing Wall Street, is that "anyone [should be able to] manipulate the numbers to compare performance." In addition, the ability to do so would be decentralized. Instead of the major power and influence being restricted to the professional investor class, ranging from security analysts to hedge fund managers, it would be accessible to all. This, of course, mirrors the democracy provided by the technology of the Internet. Roth opines in his "Transparency Now!" manifesto: "By giving everyone access to every piece of data—and making it easy to crunch—we can crowdsource regulations, creating a self-correcting financial system and unlocking new ways of measuring the market's health."

Among the proposed solutions for making that possible is the adoption of a system of tags that would create a common frame of reference. One format is what's called XBRL (extensible business reporting language). Invented by accountant Charlie Hoffman, XBRL provides universal tags that make data easy to manipulate for comparative purposes. As recommended by the NIRI, about fifty companies have already adopted the approach and filed their 10-Ks with the SEC according to that format. But this kind of "radical transparency" won't be useful for investors until the majority of public companies embrace it, or are forced to by the government.

In addition, there is the push for just-in-time financial information. Instead of bundling financial and operating data into quarterly reports and ARs, that data could be uniformly tagged and posted online 24/7. In this format the data could be transmitted to any web page, spreadsheet, or database. Because of the volatility of global economic developments, companies such as Coca-Cola have already suspended quarterly earnings guidance reports. Instead of resuming them ever again, companies might replace them with just-in-time releases of information.

But that is, or could be, in the future. Until then, financial reporting and other kinds of communications with investors have to do the best they can within the limits of the current modus operandi. This chapter provides guidelines for maximizing the value of an AR—at least at the time this handbook was published.

ROLE OF THE ANNUAL REPORT

The AR role in the process of financial reporting, as well as hands-on IR, is essentially this: It functions as the published document, required by the SEC, to be available to shareholders. What's contained in that document and how it is distributed have changed over the years. Of course, change will continue.

CONTENTS

By law, an AR must include audited statements that provide details about the performance of the public company during the past calendar year. The core of the report is what's known as the 10-K form, which details financials without containing narrative or commentary. It includes:

- Auditor's report on the financial statements
- Balance sheet
- Statement of retained earnings
- Income statement
- Cash flow statement
- Notes to the financial statements
- Accounting practices

Proxy materials on other matters relevant to or voted on by shareholders (for example, compensation) are also required to be filed with the 10-K.

In addition, there is what's sometimes referred to as the "10-K wrap." That's the narrative piece. It could be a few pages or many, chock-full of prose, photos, and other graphics or sparse with words and visuals. When ARs were big, glossy, snail-mailed publications, the contents could be thick—and expensive to produce and distribute. According to the NIRI, the median cost, excluding postage, was about $100,000.

In 2001, the New York Stock Exchange (NYSE) eliminated the shareholder, hard-copy distribution rule. The SEC still requires shareholder distribution, but it can be done in the form of a 10-K or proxy. In 2007, the SEC amended this rule to eliminate the need for snail-mailing the 10-K or proxy. All that is required is that these materials be made available on the company website and shareholders are notified that they are there. Upon request, a hard copy must be provided. The median online budget for that kind of distribution, says the NIRI, is about $5,000.

Most companies still "wrap" the numbers in a narrative, or the company's story, that is distributed primarily on the Web and in the form of a video. Hard copy is always available. The most important part of that narrative is the Letter to Shareholders.

The letter, explains Kopec, should be the personal communication of the leader, in the executive's own unique voice, about where the company has been in the past year, where it is heading, and its strategies and tactics for getting there. The objective is to transmit a strong human presence. That communicates leadership. Therefore, the letter should never be generic or boilerplate. For that reason, plenty of sweat equity is invested in planning and actually writing it. Just look at the shareholder letters from the stars in this field, such as GE and McDonald's.

The letter's tone should be candid, confident, and caring or audience-centric. In some organizational cultures, such as with a consumer-products company, the tone can be somber, funny, or ironic. Length shouldn't go beyond two pages. Increasingly, IR experts are positioning the Letter to Shareholders as the company's central branding message. The audience for this message includes:

- Security analysts
- Individual and institutional investors
- Media
- Government and nongovernmental organizations (NGOs)
- Employees
- Supply chain partners

- Communities
- Competitors

In addition to the letter, companies may (or may not) provide a smorgasbord of other material, such as descriptions, photos, graphs, or videos of products, services, customers, supply chain partners, global expansion statistics, and sales increases.

But the section of the AR receiving the closest read is the one on corporate governance: how the company is managed and controlled. That part of the AR should detail specifics—beginning with names, background information, and areas of responsibility for the board of directors, its members, and its committees. Increasingly, constituencies demand instructions on how to contact the board. If this information cannot be provided, then what must be provided is the actual name and multiple contact options for the IR leader. There's no more anonymity in this function.

This preoccupation with governance has been growing since the Enron affair. Those with a stake in the company, or considering one, understand how a compliant, politically tone-deaf, careless, or criminal board can plunge a company into scandal, litigation, or even bankruptcy. Among the issues are:

- How do the board members and its committees make decisions?
- How many members are independent of management?
- What are the policies and approval channels for management compensation, as well as compensation for board members?
- What are the policies for hiring and terminating management?
- What are the controls on Internet security and protection of intellectual property?
- How is the company audited?
- What are the policies on corporate responsibility matters such as the environment?

TALK

Digital communication makes feedback low-cost and, if managed right, plentiful. All companies have to do is open up every vehicle in IR to interactivity. There will be plenty of talk coming from all sorts of constituencies and going in all directions. Companies know they probably have made that human connection when their constituencies are talking to each other, not just with representatives from the company.

Treat each bit of input, positive and negative, as a nugget of gold. Companies with the biggest piles of this kind of gold could be the global winners in the twenty-first century.

TAKEAWAYS

- The AR will continue to change, probably significantly in the aftermath of the financial markets meltdown in 2009. The goal is to restore investor confidence in equities.
- Financial reporting was institutionalized in the early 1930s to bring about transparency. However, that only resulted in data pouring out of companies to the SEC with no standardized way of interpreting the information in comparison to information from other companies.
- One proposed reform is the implementation of standardized tags (XBRL) on all financial information. Another reform is a 24/7 release cycle versus quarterly reports and ARs.
- Digital technology has significantly reduced the cost of distributing the AR.
- In addition to the 10-K, the two most important parts of the AR are the Letter to Shareholders and the Governance Section.
- Companies must make IR communications interactive.

SECTION FOUR

MAKING IT HAPPEN

Human beings typically communicate either verbally, by the written word, or visually. Whatever form of communication, it must be supported by accurate information and knowledge that often requires considerable research and probing. The next five chapters provide a valuable primer from certified experts on how to most effectively and productively employ the spoken and written word to achieve your public relations objectives—from speechwriting to making presentations to penning op-ed pieces and undertaking reliable research.

CHAPTER

SPEECHES AS UNIQUE SIGNATURES

"I asked a political leader I had handled press relations for what he would have done differently. He answered, 'Slowed it down.' That included how he delivered speeches."

—Robert Laird

THE DELIVERED SPEECH REPRESENTS an important step in communications. That's because it gives the orator the opportunity to "say it in his or her own words" and not be interpreted. What's communicated will be part of an overall message. There is no such entity as a stand-alone speech. The speaking engagement reinforces a core message—in a unique manner.

EVERYMAN/EVERYWOMAN AS SPEAKER

This unique opportunity is not only designed for well-known leaders. The reality is that countless organizations around the world are hungry to get information, insight, and, yes, inspiration from those with proven expertise or experience. They include local service clubs such as the Rotary, trade associations, religious organizations, and special-interest groups, such as those supporting children's safety or some grassroots lobbying initiatives. Many speaking engagements will be unpaid. Some will be paid.

A little detective work is needed to open those doors. Simply investigate, on the Web, through phone calls, or through old-fashioned snail mail, what organizations welcome outside speakers, what topics they are interested in, and how to "pitch" the speaker. Some groups may require a formal proposal, including a description of the general subject, an outline of the talk, and the credentials of the speaker. Others may just close the deal over the phone. After the topic, date, and time is set, other issues—including the setup of a cocktail reception, if desired, or media coverage—can be ironed out.

THE GREAT SPEECH

How can you ensure a great speech? Great speeches come from the heart. Therefore, it's no coincidence that *authentically great speeches* are usually crafted and delivered in not-ordinary times. In periods of upheaval, crisis, and unthinkable pain, words genuinely spoken from the heart are what the nation, the company, the religious group, or the family will trust. All great speakers—Jesus Christ, Abraham Lincoln, Franklin Roosevelt, Winston Churchill, Lee Iacocca, Steve Jobs, and Barack Obama—have understood that. Our current turbulent age has all the conditions, fortunately or unfortunately, for producing years of great speeches.

Unlike many other areas of communications, the speech itself has not been significantly changed by the mainstreaming of digital technology. As Robert Laird, the former press secretary for the New York Mayor's Office, points out, one of the impacts that digitalization has had on speech writing and delivery involves the expectations of the audience. "Those listening to a speech in the twenty-first century have a short attention span," says Laird, currently a principal with The Dilenschneider Group. "That means the speech not only has to be no longer than fifteen or twenty minutes, but must also be full of memorable phrases and concrete imagery. In addition, the focus has to be kept to no more than three key points." Laird also stresses that "audiences expect interactivity; that is, being part of the show. That means leaving plenty of time for questions and answers."

Laird has one more observation. And it's ironic. From his conversations with political leaders, including a former New York mayor, Laird has found that slow plays best. When he asked the ex-mayor what he would have done differently in the many speeches he had delivered, the stunner of a reply was: "Slow it down." To illustrate his point, the mayor vividly recalled one incident. He gave a keynote address that was televised. When he got home he asked his wife, "Honey, what did you think?" She answered, "You spoke much too quickly. I couldn't make out much of the content."

Although the writing and the delivery of the speech, in essence, remain an old-fashioned art, digital also has a major impact on the reach of a speech. In real time, speeches can be video streamed around the world. As the speaker is addressing the audience, live bloggers, including tweeters in that very audience, may be instantly deconstructing the tone and content and sending brief thumbs-up or thumbs-down reviews on what they are hearing. A video/audio version of the speech can also eventually appear on the speaker's website. And for days, or even weeks, strong opinions regarding the speech can be bouncing around the Web.

PREPARING THE SPEECH

With that kind of influence possible and probable, speakers and those assisting them should be investing considerable resources in preparing the formal speech. You will come across other areas in this book that offer an analysis of delivery fundamentals for speeches, presentations, and media interviews, and for presenting oneself on the job market and in developing new business.

STEP 1: AUDIENCE DUE DILIGENCE

The speech begins with the audience. If the sponsoring organization is, for example, the Detroit Economic Club, it might provide audience specifications, so the speaker would know the audience is made up of senior-level executives, median age 45; members of the United Auto Workers (UAW); federal, state, and local government leaders; and members of the media, general and trade. Across the board, the prime audience concern is the future of the economy in the Midwest.

Those specs, just like the traditional job description, relay nothing about what is necessary to succeed at the task. It is up to the speakers' staff, or the speakers themselves, to play the role of journalist and/or anthropologist, digging, interviewing, researching, and also recognizing the emotional temperature of their audience. Then they must create a speech that synthesizes those components. In their heads should be blaring some kind of provocative headline: "Whistling past the graveyard." "Stuck in 1980." "Waking up angry." Or "Hit bottom, ready to change."

This is hands-on work. The numbers from a poll may be useful to peruse, but polls only give crude snapshots of opinion at a certain time. And those opinions might not accurately reflect what's in the hearts and minds of people. Those interviewed might have just been laid off and buried themselves behind a fortress of unavailability, or they might have just won a major new account and are unduly optimistic.

The journalist in most communicators and speakers should push them to want to be on the scene. There can be a payoff in wandering the streets; buttonholing government, industrial, union, academic, and church leaders; starting up conversations with patrons at the local Mickey D's, the unemployment office, the car dealership, and country clubs. Mining for data in this way can bring insights, from which can come God's plenty of other speeches, opinion-editorials targeted to media such as the *Wall Street Journal* and *Forbes*, video scripts, podcasts, postings on the organization's intranet or the speaker's blog, even texting opportunities to employees. It may even be a gold mine for brainstorming in product meetings or customer-service reviews, for instance.

If you are unable to conduct this "due diligence" in person because the venue of the speech might be in a distant state or even overseas, then read the media in those locations to derive a list of first contacts who can be reached by e-mail or phone.

STEP 2: CONNECTING THE DOTS

Next, speakers should review the notes on what has turned up. They have to ask themselves as well as their trusted advisers, What's the story here? There's always a story line that resonates. It might be that people are excited about beginning new or that the obstacle to new beginnings is cutting loose the dreams of another era. From this story emerges the message. That might be, as with Barack Obama, "Yes We Can."

The message should be kept simple. Jesus's words have endured for centuries because they capture a universal truth in "short form." So did Gandhi's words. Will we ever recall even a line from Castro's three-hour rants?

The message is the DNA that determines what kind of speech will be born. That's the beauty of a clear message. Like a brand, it will make all the other decisions easier.

STEP 3: THE MESSAGE, THE EMOTIONAL CONTENT

There has to be an emotional connection between the message being delivered and the speaker. The message has to mean something very personal. That's why stories, anecdotes, and striking imagery are the building blocks of great speeches.

Because he was an actor in an industry that told stories visually, Ronald Reagan knew that instinctively. And what came from his mouth, body language, and facial gestures seemed to communicate genuine conviction.

The tough part for the speaker is to sift through so many options. We are emotionally hardwired. A great deal resonates with us on a feeling level. The issue is: *What feeling, story, or lesson can transport the speaker from mere human to healer, visionary, national cheerleader, and/or nuts-and-bolts fixer?*

To help figure that out, speakers might review their own lives for what messages moved them to change, dream bigger, or stick with the program until the miracle happened. Then they have to figure out how those messages were positioned and packaged.

A noted industrial leader attending the World Economic Forum in Davos, Switzerland, once told a panel about a dying alcoholic who served to keep him sober: "This man and his family communicated through their suffering the choice open to me. Perhaps their mission in life was to save the rest of us alcoholics from a similar needless death."

Another road that is helpful to travel is attending or viewing videos of services in houses of worship. It's said that Bill Clinton cut his rhetorical teeth on the feeling, language, and gestures of the African-American church in the South. It's no surprise that most people turn to their ministers, priests, rabbis, and Buddhist monks when they need to sort things out.

STEP 4: ORGANIZATION

Organizing the speech is the next step. How to start? Gee-whiz, cute, or funny won't cut it. The most effective way to introduce oneself to the audience is by focusing on them. This was always true, but is especially so in a digital age when all relationships are horizontal. The audience's everyman/everywoman is as important a human being as the chief executive officer of Ford Motor Company or the Queen of England.

The tone? Irony and parody work well in the modern age. In the Great Depression, a comic genius like Charlie Chaplin stole people's hearts because he understood the complex human feelings driving people. Chaplin was a master of ironic distancing (*The Gold Rush*) and of using parody to show the stupidities of the culture (*Modern Times*).

After the opening—and it is fine to start out slowly—there's the age-old speech-giving tradition of:

- Telling the audience what you are going to tell them
- Telling them what you said you would
- Telling them again what you have just told them

That format holds because it carries the message efficiently and effectively.

Here's an example of that approach:

> Tonight, we're going to find out about a miracle that wasn't supposed to happen. And almost didn't! *(telling what you are there to speak about)*
>
> Jersey City, New Jersey, had always been a joke. During the 1970s and 1980s, it wasn't even relevant enough to remain a joke. Then some out-of-the-box entrepreneurs noticed something: Jersey City was a short PATH train ride from Manhattan. *(telling the audience what you said you would)*
>
> Tonight, we experienced together how one miracle happened. Now, we can go on to apply this experience to planting the seeds, and nurturing the fragile growth, for other miracles. *(reiterating what you just told the audience)*

STEP 5: BUILDING THROUGH RHYTHM, IMAGERY, WORDS

Speeches are targeted toward the ear, not the eye. The ear is a very limited organ. That's why speakers have to make clear what they are referring to; what they are referring to a second time; and what they are referring to a third time. A speech cannot refer to "he" or "she" or "it." There is always a specific name given. The audience does not, and should not, have the text in front of them. If the speaker refers to Barack Obama three times, then his name, title, or another specific identifying reference should be used.

Of course, the content and delivery of any speech will be significantly influenced by the audience to whom it is directed. But it is important to remember that speeches are not, by and large, meant to be conversations, although certain conversational elements can, occasionally, be employed for effect. Human conversations tend to be rambling, cliché-ridden, ungrammatical, unconnected, and replete with incomplete sentences. A rare charismatic personality such as Sarah Palin, thanks to admiring audiences, can sometimes pull off this conversational speaking style. But she was still often ridiculed by the media for repetitious use of colloquialisms like "You betcha," "Yup," and "Gonna"—not to mention her signature winking.

Speeches that have power, a strong message, and the ability to sway and resonate with audiences should be formal, informative, structured, coherent, grammatically correct, and, of course, well-written—perhaps even eloquent, using memorable language if the speech-giver or writer has the talent to shape such words.

That's why Barack Obama's speeches in the last presidential campaign were received so enthusiastically while his opponent often sounded flat and uninspiring. Humor also helps any speech, no matter how serious the subject matter. Many good speeches commence with a relevant, amusing anecdote or joke—ideally, one that is not already an oft-told tale. Repetition, for emphasis, is yet another valuable rhetorical device. Appropriate pauses to let an idea sink in are helpful, too, as are trademark phrases that differentiate the recognizable style of the speaker.

STEP 6: BREAKING OPEN TO THE AUDIENCE

Now comes the interactive part. In a digital age, this is where the rubber meets the road. Speakers must be prepared for all kinds of questions and comments. Old-line politeness has been replaced by the outspokenness of the Millennials. This generation controls many of the most popular digital applications. They also tend to be profane, candid to the point of cruelty, and willing to inflict public shame on anyone who isn't measuring up to their standards.

The worst can be prevented if speakers know who they are; know what they know; know what they do not know; know the value of a real heated conversation; and know they, as speakers, are there to learn. When speakers disagree with audience members, they should stick to their guns. If they see merit in what the audience member is saying, then they should open the door to the rest of the audience by going to the mat on the issue. If the discussion lapses into the vulgar, then ground rules have to be set down. Pushing back is the most effective and respected way to maintain control over the message.

In terms of interactivity, the speech and question-and-answer experiences are merely the beginning of messaging. Speakers can reinforce their message and extend interactivity by providing the audience with ways to reach them later. That might be publicizing e-mail addresses; URLs for websites, blogs, and micrologs; and links for posting excerpts of the speech and the question-and-answer portion on YouTube. In addition, speakers might reflect and amplify on the speech using their own sites, podcasts, company intranets, op-eds in top-tier media, articles in trade publications, and presentations to the board of directors.

With influential outlets so available and the low costs involved, thanks to digitalization, a speech can be widely and profitably merchandised to many audiences besides those in the hall.

FAILURE'S NOT TO BE WASTED

It sometimes happens that a certain speech didn't come off well, the question-and-answer part seemed unduly harsh, and the media coverage was mediocre. But this lemon could and should be turned into lemonade. Negative learning tends to be powerful. The crisis of embarrassment opens us up to observing our behavior and assumptions. The hope of preventing a similar future ordeal allows us to do extensive course correction.

Incidentally, quite aside from speech-making do-overs, the most astounding career leaps have come from failure. Think Winston Churchill, Lee Iacocca, Steve Jobs, Bill Clinton, and Larry Summers. Also consider this: There could be a book opportunity in recounting one's moment of truth and the whole new journey taken. Or even a lucrative franchise created, focusing on helping to reinvent those who stumble.

TAKEAWAYS

- Speeches are an individual signature, the unique opportunity to reinforce an overall message.
- Everyman/everywoman can, and should, take advantage of the opportunity to speak.
- The payoff from doing the speech right can be almost infinite; a speech and its by-products can be recycled through other media, ranging from print opinion-editorials to YouTube excerpts.
- Failure is the beginning of success.

CHAPTER

COMPOSING PRESENTATIONS

"Presentations are how we sell points of view, products, services, and ourselves."

—Joan Avagliano

....

THE GENIUS OF CHARLES SCHULZ, creator of the comic strip *Peanuts*, was that he understood the awesome power—negative and positive—that comes from how people present themselves. That power overrides all intentions.

Take *Peanuts* character Lucy. Psychologists might conclude that in her heart of hearts, Lucy wants friends. She wants to be less lonesome. She wants to make a difference. But she presents herself as intrusive, mouthy, and outrageous. That drives people away, creates conflict, and makes so many others miserable. If Schulz were doing *Peanuts* today, Lucy would be in presentation rehab.

As chief administrative officer at The Dilenschneider Group, Joan Avagliano deals every day with folks who want something from her or the agency founder. Yet, she observes, "most [people] present themselves poorly. They seem clueless that presentations are how we sell points of view, products, services, and ourselves—and that they give us control. Present well and it doesn't matter what's happening in the economy and who's the competition."

This chapter concentrates on the ingredients of effective presentations and the pitfalls that lead too many presenters to fail. In a digital era, the standards for presentations—some call them "performance art"—are higher than they were when a gee-whiz PowerPoint presentation (PPP) could close a deal or a highly focused interview could snag a job offer. Now, there are the digitally generated demands for authenticity, simplicity, brevity, speed, entertainment, and anything-but-vanilla presentations.

In pre-digital times, the conventional wisdom was that the world gives presenters perhaps about four minutes to make a favorable impression. With the rhythms of the Internet embedded in the global psyche, that allowance probably has been radically compressed. Attention must be gotten faster. When that doesn't happen, it may never come from that particular audience. The presenter is a marked person. That mark shouts: boring, inept, unfocused, self-absorbed, preachy, top-down, and/or complicated.

In composing presentations, be they PowerPoint, a job cover letter, a podcast, an on-the-feet sales pitch, or an interview for a position or promotion, what are the musts for effectiveness? Here's how the game gets played in a world shaped by digital.

AUDIENCE

It all begins with the audience. Presenting is about them, not the presenter. That's why it is professional suicide to use generic material instead of custom-making whatever you may be pitching for the particular person or people on the receiving end. Sure, that's work. It may demand fine-tuning or even overhauling the pattern PPP or cover letter for each individual situation. But that's the only way. Those who either don't realize that or won't invest the effort are the ones making pitch after pitch, applying for position after position, and not getting results. They are also the ones on the Internet who are ignored.

Lawyers, whose presentations on paper or on their feet have high stakes for clients, are especially sensitive to this concept of audience. That's why jury selection is an important part of litigation. In addition, attorneys analyze the format of a brief preferred by a judge before submitting their own motion.

When testifying before congressional committees about pending legislation, a regulation, or abuse, smart attorneys deconstruct all the key constituencies, ranging from the members of the committee or subcommittee to the public to the media. Then they frame their remarks to have the greatest impact on, and the least downside for, the most influential among them. Since controversy can get attention and function as a persuasive device, shrewd lawyers won't necessarily steer clear of that tactic. Legal luminary Alan Dershowitz has made a career out of defending controversial clients and causes.

How to find out about the audience? Naturally empathetic individuals do the best. They can transcend their own preoccupations in order to provide what the audience expects, needs, and wants. Here are the basic items to research:

- How is the industry, company, or leader doing? If they are in positive territory, they likely want to be recognized for that. If problem-ridden, they would be open to solutions, offered respectfully and even humbly. Classic sales technique calls for locating the pain and addressing it as a healer, not a hungry go-getter.
- What are the underlying fears? The best persuaders are those who intuitively pick up on the vulnerabilities of others and help those people feel whole. When he was in the Senate, Lyndon Johnson excelled at detecting awkwardness and loneliness in fellow senators. He rose to the top.
- What's the hierarchy of needs? Figure out the one, two, or three things that matter most to the audience. That could be saving money. Or it could be a combination of saving money and still looking great. No presentation can, or should, address all needs.
- Who makes the decisions to purchase? Who influences them? Those are the people to pitch to. Do a Google search on them.
- What are the formative or milestone experiences of the group? Employment issues? Launching and operating wildly successful enterprises? That's the emotional content to embed in the presentation.

MESSAGE

Once the audience becomes transparent to the presenter, the next step is struggling with the right message. For example, your message could be, "I get results," or "Hire me," or "No manager who uses us as a vendor was ever fired."

All words, all graphics, all that's implied but unsaid in the presentation must communicate that message. Therefore, there's no temptation to waste the audience's time by going off on tangents. There should be complete focus on transmitting the message "I get results." Here is an actual application letter I received not too long ago that can be a good model:

Dear Mr. Dilenschneider:

I read your company's recent "help-wanted" advertisement for an associate with great interest and mounting eagerness and determination. I say this because I know of the reputation enjoyed by the firm and would be honored to join your team.

First, and foremost, permit me to state that I am a very focused, ambitious, results-driven young public relations professional who is, by nature, a team player and, equally important, a self-starter and not a clock-watcher. I have never needed someone looking over my shoulder to assure that I'm hard at work. I also like to think of myself as someone who can think "out-of-the-box."

I am likewise proud of my work and accomplishments at [name of firm] where I served for over 22 months until last May after graduating with honors from [name of college], majoring in English and editing the college's twice-weekly newspaper. Although the editor, I also worked with our student business manager to attract important new advertising from local merchants.

Unfortunately, as you may have read, [name of agency] took a huge hit, client-wise, as a result of the current recession and subsequently instituted a sweeping downsizing. It was, basically, a question of "last one hired, first one fired"—and quite understandable under the circumstances.

As an aspiring PR media specialist, I would add that I am a so-called Digital Native, familiar with all of the new media and how they work in the new world of corporate communicating. However, I also gained considerable knowledge and experience about placements with the more traditional media during my 22-month tenure at [name of agency].

A formal, more detailed resume including some samples of my writing and placements are enclosed.

Thank you for your time. Needless to add, I hope I may have the opportunity to meet you personally.

Very cordially,

Jane Doe

Note that in her letter, the applicant did not include all of the specifics about her job, other professional experiences, education, awards, memberships on boards, etc. That detailed information should be in the formal resume and doesn't belong in the cover letter.

P.S. Jane got the job.

UNIQUE POSITIONING

This is a period of glut in just about every human undertaking—from leadership to journalism to making brands of candy bars. To even get on the radar screen, one has to find a unique positioning. In short, vanilla is not selling this season.

Presenters have to do an inventory on what they are offering that the competition isn't. That could be youth in a troubled, aging, conservative political movement; fluency in Mandarin for a start-up that wants to expand globally; or a combination of youth and experience in politics. Increasingly, with so much talent on the market, determining a unique positioning requires imagination.

One unemployed public relations pro decided she would package her working-class background as a form of value-added. So she created, on the Web, the notion of blue-collar chic. Mission accomplished. On that platform, she attracted enough interest to launch a communications boutique based on what the common man is looking for. Clients wanting to reach that common man come to her.

An independent filmmaker, who had lost all his money in the Bernie Madoff con, put himself out there as someone who knew how to get the job done cheaply—and brilliantly. With nothing more to lose, he could take the kind of creative risks he didn't dare do when he had a brand name and wealth to protect.

With out-of-the-box approaches, there is no limit on how presenters can make themselves stand out. A world turned upside down is looking for those who took the road less traveled and wound up better off than where the status quo would have taken them.

INTEGRITY

No one trusts. Yet everyone longs to trust. Trust is the component necessary to get things done through other people. Shrewd presenters give audiences reason to trust them. Explicitly and implicitly they broadcast integrity. Wasn't that how Barack Obama won Campaign '08?

Integrity gets built just like everything else in a presentation: through tone and content. The tone is self-assured but concerned with the audience. In press conferences, Obama indicated he knew his worth: What he represented as a person and leader could provide America with the path to economic security. But his content didn't overpromise. It stayed within the realm of the possible and probable. Twenty-eight years earlier, back in Campaign '80, Ronald Reagan could discuss "Morning in America" when dealing with the media. Obama couldn't. What he could offer was much more limited. He knew he was dealing with a trust factor that was very different from what it had been in Reagan's time.

Here are some recommendations on establishing trust:

- Listen before starting. Those are the precious minutes when it may be possible to engage the employer, prospect, or board of directors in a casual conversation. That provides the opportunity for them to connect with the presenter on their terms. And that's the platform for trust. People choose to trust—or not trust.
- Draw parallels between others' obstacles, setbacks, and failures and your own. Suggest solutions. That has been a standard Steve Jobs tactic. Suffering has become a marketable commodity.
- Admit what you don't know and promise that you will find that out. Keep the promise.
- Listen after wrapping up. That reinforces a sense of caring.
- Deliver what you promise.

MIRRORING

Another basic of sales is mirroring the prospect. If the audience is conservative, then those making the pitch should be conservative in dress, concepts used, allusions, graphics, and language. This information about the audience can be obtained by research or simply a quick take when meeting the prospect in person or on the phone.

Mirroring is an ongoing process, too. Presenters are completely attuned to how the audience is responding—every second. If the members of the board of directors seem anxious when the profit-decline numbers are put on screen, then the presenter increases the gravitas. Eventually, the tone and content should shift to more optimism. If the board members seem bored, then the presenter can empathize with the boredom—and turn it into an advantage. "I realize this might be something you have heard many times," the presenter says. "But what's different is that no one in the industry is approaching this as a distinct niche."

To mirror, a presentation should be loosely structured. That's the danger with a set-in-stone medium such as PPP. It's not configured to be continually aligned with audience response. Far better might be having talking points, along with an easel, blank flip chart, and Magic Marker. In that way, key material can be reinforced visually, depending on what the audience indicates it finds compelling.

Mirroring is the most effective way to enhance control of any presentation or interview. By becoming in sync with the decision maker, the presenter creates the space to put forth persuasive facts, examples, personality traits, and suggestions.

SIMPLIFICATION

Dense is dumb. That's the shorthand way of saying that presentations have to be totally accessible. Simplification has always worked with human beings. Think back to how compelling and persuasive Jesus's parables are. They're simple in concept.

This mandate for simplification is even more the situation with the Internet. With so much free material available and more coming online every second, there's ramped-up competition to get and keep attention. That's why digital communicators who simplify in writing headlines, leads, and the rest of the copy endure. Think Matt Drudge of the DrudgeReport.com, who's been around since Bill Clinton was president.

The Heath brothers, Chip and Dan, wrote a useful book, *Made to Stick: Why Some Ideas Survive and Others Die.* In this book, they reference the "Duh?" test, whereby presenters learn to extract the density and create a pull force by looking at the content they've created and asking: Would bright fourteen-year-olds say "Duh" if I showed them this presentation? Or would they find it worth considering for a few minutes? In this era of short attention spans, we are all bright fourteen-year-olds.

ENTERTAINMENT

Never underestimate the audience's desire to be entertained. However, having a pitch that includes entertaining elements has always been a high-risk venture. The connection with the audience, timing, tone, and content have to be just right. That risk can be managed through the use of irony rather than humor or wit.

Irony is widely accepted nowadays because it creates emotional distance between what is and how it can be perceived. "What is," or the reality of a situation, is often scary, unpleasant, tragic. Therefore, irony provides the audience with a sense of control—and an instant rapport with the presenter. Here is an example of a job applicant (JA) using irony in an interview:

JA: Ironically, when I was laid off at Company X, I gained the confidence to trust my instincts. In a contract sales assignment for Company Y, I brought in more than two million in new revenue in five months—effortlessly. My gut told me: Pitch the price, not the product attributes.

Employer: But weren't the prospects interested in what differentiated your product from others?

JA: That's another irony. The product was perceived as a me-too. I didn't go there and attempt to change that perception. I hammered price.

Employer: What can you do for us—with your golden gut?

Irony has the ability to disarm. The audience becomes less guarded—and more trusting.

TAKEAWAYS

- Presentations function as part of the sales process. What's being sold could be a product, service, brand name, or the self.
- Presentations done well give control to the presenter, no matter what's happening in the economy or who the competition is. Remember: It's the presenter and the audience—a closed universe. That's it. It is performance art with very high stakes.
- The focus in a presentation is on the audience, be it the one employer who can make a job offer, or the client who can award a multimillion-dollar contract.
- Set scripts or approaches lose audiences, as well they should. Custom-make everything, from tone to content.
- Vanilla isn't selling this season. Differentiation provides a compelling reason for decision makers to choose the presenter who takes the road less traveled. Remember: The status quo hasn't been working well for a while now.
- Build trust, before, during, and after presentations.

CHAPTER

TALK—FORMAL OR FAMILIAR

"Talk is not 'just talk.' Everything which comes out of our mouth, as well as our body language and facial gestures, sends messages. It's our responsibility to control those messages."

—BOB BERKOWITZ

TALK HAS NEVER BEEN CHEAP. In digital times, its value is increasing exponentially. After all, as *The Cluetrain Manifesto* stresses: Markets are conversations. Word-of-mouth or word-of-mouse can break or make a career, product, service, or company brand name.

This isn't new. Back in ancient times, talk came with a high price. Saying the wrong things in the wrong way cost Socrates his life. On the other hand, the right words uttered on board ship helped make Odysseus a hero. What is new is that in this era of declining trust in institutions, people are putting more trust in what others like them are saying.

Obviously, the goal is to say what will help a career or a product or a brand name, and in a way that maximizes its echo in a world that, thanks to the Internet, operates virally. This chapter presents recommendations for how to achieve that goal and minimize disasters such as putting in play the wrong echo.

TALK NOT JUST TALK

When Bob Berkowitz, principal with The Dilenschneider Group, coaches global leaders in public speaking, he advises them about the importance of strategic planning and execution—or what he refers to as the "responsibility to control messages." Leaders err on the side of caution. Fools on the side of spontaneity.

Unfortunately, many Millennials may wake up one day and realize that by their ramblings on social networks they have become the economy's fools. Since the 1970s, when counterculture's emphasis on personal self-expression and self-disclosure became something good, verbal restraint has been viewed as inauthentic. However, the public aspect and the viral quality of digital media, including the wide availability of cheap digital tools, make the cult of the "unedited me" dangerous.

The old-fashioned reality is that being able to be candid and confide, as parents always said, is a luxury. That's why human beings hunger for those few authentic, intimate relationships that are possible and are devastated when they end, as with divorce or death. The role of psychotherapists, executive coaches, and attorneys is to provide (for a fee) that guaranteed privacy and safety—or rented intimacy.

This chapter demonstrates how to talk in a strategic manner without coming across as excessively guarded or evasive. There are phrases, body language, and facial expressions that establish quick bonds with others and yet insulate the speaker from verbal recklessness.

What kinds of messages does talk transmit? The number is infinite. At the top of the list is the raw data on which those listening will make decisions about the speaker. They decide on the speaker's integrity, social class, education, confidence, expertise, worldview, and more. Also, what's being transmitted could include unique positioning and packaging of information, insight, and inspiration. It's those qualities of a message that can land the job, account, or political win, or bring unexpected success to a new product or service. During Campaign '08, the Obama team understood the power of a fresh message custom-made for trying times.

If there is only one guideline that readers take away from this book it is this: Know your audience. Remember, human beings come to conversations with a complex genetic makeup, past experiences, and current hopes and worries. All of that programs them to "hear" what's said the way they want or need to. After a while, speakers develop a sixth sense about types of people and what to say or not say to them. But even then, until the audience is a known entity, speakers will tread carefully verbally, both in tone and content.

To create that emotional connect while being appropriately guarded, speakers can use mainstream or profession-specific buzz, open body language, and friendly facial expressions. Those serve as the universal language of communicating while maintaining a zone of privacy.

The migration from controlled conversation to more familiar will happen as speakers gain more experience with individual listeners and the types they represent. That's why politicians who win elections don't rely entirely on polls. They go out there and find out on their own what's on the minds and in the hearts of constituents. Those applying for jobs or courting accounts will research the organization and do a Google search of the decision makers. However, they must still enter the interviewing situation alert to specific signals coming from the listeners. Talk is a process, never a set script.

TALK AS SERIOUS BUSINESS

This sensitivity to talk as totally strategic became mainstream, at least among professionals, in the late 1980s, when academic linguist Deborah Tannen's breakthrough research into the correlation between speaking style and content and success was published in the book *That's Not What I Meant!* In the mid-1990s, Tannen added to those insights in a follow-up book, *Talking from 9 to 5*. She focused on ordinary conversations and their impact on an individual's professional advancement. Her readers got it: Talk is serious business.

What Tannen spelled out was that professionals aren't just being assessed on their formal addresses to the board of directors, the keynote speeches at a professional society, or the content of structured job interviews. The scorekeepers who matter—those who can purchase, promote, hire—are continually busy giving grades when people assume they are "just talking." In the Tannen world of talk, nothing is simply what is uttered. And rarely will it be treated as private. In fact, in digital times, that's expanded to: Count on every conversation possibly being made public. The line between private and public is so blurred that Millennials probably don't realize a clear one used to exist. Only the naïve assume any utterance is "off the record."

But Tannen didn't stop at the direct and predictable relationship between talk and upward mobility. She also dug down into how factors such as gender shaped how professionals talked, and how that in turn determined whether their career runway would be long or short.

What Tannen documented was that a so-called feminine conversational style could and usually would hold women back. In meetings, at least back in the 1980s and even into the mid-1990s, women tended to frame their suggestions and observations in questions. That style made them appear unsure of themselves. In delivering criticism, they could be so indirect and gentle that the miscreant didn't understand what was wrong and how to fix it. Mutual frustration would follow and the female manager could get a bad rep as being difficult to work with.

NEW WINNERS, LOSERS

Unfortunately, those who followed Tannen's thinking tended to overcorrect. The feminine style gave way to the Professional Woman, or worse. That was no way to communicate, not for women and not even for men.

Currently, women, but also men, are struggling to find the right voice for these changing times. As this book is being written, arrogant, entirely top-down approaches seem increasingly ineffective. But those styles could return as the world economy grows quickly again.

Those who can discern the right style for the times are the new winners. They include Secretary of State Hillary Clinton, former Alaska governor Sarah Palin, corporate executive Pat Russo, financial literary essayist Nassim Nicholas Taleb, and lawyer/author Philip Howard. They have the gift of fusing strategic intent with a conversational style that resonates with their audiences.

THE BASICS

There are many and diverse forms of talk. On the formal side there are speeches, presentations, web seminars, testimonials, media conferences, organizational announcements, breaking news reports, lectures, entertainment, interviewing, eulogies, and prayers. On the less formal end, there are intimate conversations, elevator chats, social platitudes, gossiping, rumormongering, advice giving, therapeutic explorations, confessions, outbursts, and rants.

What they all have in common are universal or basic principles about what is effective in transmitting a message. Here Berkowitz, a former AP Radio, CNN, and NBC editor-reporter, shares the basic guidelines:

- *Customize the message.* Everything begins with the message. And the message has to begin with who the listeners are. The message to a working-class audience might be about jobs with security, higher pay, and more benefits. To professionals, the message might be about structuring employment that ensures developing marketable or transferable skills. Each message has to be custom-made. No one size fits all.
- *Convey confidence but humility.* This is the tone used by speakers who have endured over whole careers. It's the dominant style in late 2009. Steve Forbes, although not a master of charisma, understands the power of self-assurance mixed with an openness to learn. This is known as "presence." It's palpable. Anyone willing to try can develop presence. Onetime folk hero Lee Iacocca made an investment in improving his speaking ability; wherever he was scheduled to speak, it was said, he would arrive at the venue a day early to practice, practice, practice.
- *Provide a learning experience.* Content is king, always has been. The difference now is that speakers who cannot provide value in talk will be ignored, then isolated. There's no space for recollections of "ancient mariners" in insight-starved, fast-moving times. Society wants/needs to learn. With so much that's new and not necessarily positive happening to so many, first-person narratives that disclose lessons are wildly in demand.
- *Maintain eye contact, but not in an aggressive manner.* There is a fine line between being engaged and intensity. Don't cross over into hotness. Most listeners can't tolerate the level of heat. It's claimed that singer Judy Garland lost her television show because she presented herself as too hot in what the network executives wanted to be a cool medium.

- *Use body language and facial expressions as second and third languages.* In such a performance-sensitive world, those who only speak one language are at a distinct disadvantage. It is just as important to know that different cultures may perceive those languages differently. In some parts of the world, smiling could be perceived as being overly familiar.
- *Care, and show it.* Empathy doesn't mean agreement with a point of view. It simply means understanding the viewpoints of others and respecting those who have them. One of the most primitive needs of mankind is to be understood.
- *Don't aim to win.* This advice is especially relevant when in a hostile or uncomfortable setting, such as when testifying before Congress or in a meeting with a narcissistic boss. Play a careful hand verbally and hope to just emerge not looking bad. It's a law of interaction that those with the most power establish the definition of the situation. It's reckless to attempt to buck that. There's an art to knowing how to avoid becoming ensnared with crazy bosses. If you won't be missed in a meeting or if showing up at a function isn't imperative, you might consider not becoming a participant in no-win situations.
- *Listen.* Most people fail to spot and seize opportunity because they were talking or preparing their response, not listening. Way back in the 1930s, the granddaddy of public speaking, Dale Carnegie, observed that listeners get reputations for being brilliant conversationalists—and everyone wants them around.
- *Be truthful.* Digital trails make falsehoods easy to pick up on, and even easier to let the world know about.
- *Remain within your area of expertise.* Medical doctors should not attempt to be legal experts, unless they are.
- *Admit what you don't know.* One option is to offer to investigate the question and get back to the questioner. Speculating makes you appear insecure; that is, as if needing to come across as more knowledgeable than you are. Forecasting is fine, as long as it's within your field. Oprah might be perceived as being too ambitious for ratings if she made unilateral predictions on the economy.

- *Frame weaknesses as strengths.* The out-of-work job applicant communicates hunger as an asset. The youth with no experience pushes high energy, technical literacy, no family responsibilities, and an ability to be trained as assets.
- *Keep it as brief as possible.* No listener wants or needs the whole story, with every detail. The rule of thumb is to leave the listener craving more.
- *Remain calm; that is, in control.* When listeners realize they are powerless to get the speaker worked up, they will move on to someone who is more reactive. If you are found to be wrong about something, admit it, do a sincere mea culpa, and move on. When misunderstood, attempt to clarify on the spot. If that doesn't do the trick, there are ways to again make one's point afterward. There is also the option of just letting it drop.
- *Never correct a superior in public.* The superior's lead should be followed, in public. This is key performance art. Deviate from that script and listeners will be confused—and uncomfortable.
- *Make a two-way conversation possible, no matter what the medium.* Provide audiences with question-and-answer time; tell them how to e-mail or text-message you; share URLs of individual or company sites.
- *Practice.* Job applicants who role-play what-if scenarios feel more confident and, consequently, tend to perform better.

THE CURSE OF SELF-CONSCIOUSNESS

Since Tannen published her books on ordinary talk, there have been incentives and funds to further research that field. One question that was especially compelling was why speakers who did all the right things—that is, who follow the guidelines as Berkowitz recommends—performed subpar. A common hypothesis was that they overprepared.

No, answered University of Chicago psychologist Sian L. Beilock. From her research, discussed in the February/March 2009 edition of *Scientific American Mind* in Elizabeth Svoboda's "How to Avoid Choking Under Pressure," she concluded that failure, or "choking" in front of an audience, was the result of a speaker being self-conscious or reflecting on oneself.

For example, executives giving an address to employees may halt midstream, turn inward, and ask themselves: "How am I doing?" That breaks their concentration and the speech's flow. Usually, it's lost forever, at least in that presentation. Whether it's a keynote speech or job interview or marriage proposal to a lover, stay in the moment or the zone. Remain outside with the audience, not inside with the self.

Any kind of self-absorption while talking will prove to be a distraction. Talking is a public context. That's why those who talk to themselves are perceived as mentally unbalanced.

Preoccupation with what's going on inside oneself has always impaired performance. Political leader Barney Frank disclosed that he emerged as a force in shaping legislation only after he outed himself as a gay man. Before that, he was locked inside himself, attempting to conceal his secret and obsessed with who might know it. No surprise, St. Francis's prayer for self-forgetfulness is becoming increasingly popular.

THE WORLD AS STAGE

There are diverse "stages" on which to speak. As sociologist Erving Goffman argued in the late 1950s, each stage requires a custom-made performance. Goffman observed that even the uneducated butcher in the French provinces understood the necessity of having a different face, along with different words and body language, to present to all the faces out there.

In his classic *The Presentation of Self in Everyday Life*, Goffman describes this device as "a cuticle" humans must acquire when "in contact with the air." It is a protective stance. Not continually creating personas for diverse situations is bound to result in being labeled anything from a loser to a sufferer of Asperger's syndrome.

Violating conventional social expectations in verbal communications is high risk. That's why those who engage in this strategy, such as stand-up comics like the late Lenny Bruce and muckraking television anchors like Lou Dobbs, can achieve success—at least in the circles important to them. High risk, high reward.

Immigrant ethnic groups who perceive themselves as having nothing to lose in American mainstream culture usually choose to ignore social convention. Their energy may go into interacting with "their own kind" versus conforming. Eventually, aspects of that strategy, such as speaking their native language in public and at work, end up becoming a pressing and controversial national issue, as it has in the United States. Every struggling group and individual has to weigh the possible payoffs from not following the dominant script.

TALK IN VISUAL MEDIA

Most talk takes place in a visual setting. Two coworkers run into each other in the restroom. The executive delivers remarks to an audience simultaneously in person and on a video feed. Excerpts are leaked on YouTube. Testimony is given live in the U.S. House of Representatives before a committee and the media. The mother of a victim of the peanut-butter contamination lawsuit appears on a television talk show.

Obviously, success in performance transcends words. There are certain nonverbal factors that cannot be controlled. They include:

- *Lighting and other aspects of the setting.* Sitting in front of an office panel or the House of Representatives can make the speaker appear old, malevolent, or evasive. That can't be changed. The impacts, though, can be reduced. Some ambitious professionals import coaches and other kinds of experts into their workplaces to analyze factors such as dress, makeup, body language, or even another speaking style that may help them come across better in those environments.

- *Camera angles.* If speakers are not on the same political wavelength as those with the power over the camera, the odds are they will be at a visual disadvantage. Therefore, the question is whether or not it is useful or necessary to accept the invitation to begin with.

- *Hardball questions and comments.* Speakers should expect them, but learn to control how they frame their responses. That includes being sympathetic with the point of view; remaining calm; avoiding stiff body language or a tightening of facial muscles; restating the matter without appearing evasive; moving the discussion to the solution; admitting an error; apologizing and discussing the fix; presenting the facts; and thanking the interviewer for raising the issue.

Other factors affecting success or failure in performance are within the speaker's control. For instance:

- The message is partly communicated through every aspect of appearance, from hairstyle to color of shirt. Elton John is sending the message of outrageousness and looks the part. The executive's message of credibility, expertise, power, and influence is best transmitted with conventional business attire.

- Body language and facial expressions should be prescreened by a visual-media expert who can detect tics and quirks.

- Eye contact should be maintained with the interviewer or audience, not the camera.

- Professional coaching may be necessary. In an unnatural or hostile setting, the hosts have the advantage. The best of bad outcomes will occur if one doesn't try to score points. Maintain dignity. There is no mercy to be dealt out, so don't request any. Coaching can assist with enduring this ordeal and exiting in the best manner possible.

- When possible, speakers should bring appropriate props, such as their own team members, products, and YouTube excerpts. Steve Jobs and Bill Gates are masters here. Props can expand the interview's power by acting as a pull force with the audience.

BEING DIFFERENT

Being perceived as being "different" or "the other" can present disadvantages in talk. Even in this day and age, controversy about winning personas for females in the workplace still rage on and on. Even such mundane issues as high heels versus sensible shoes are highly debated. So is the use of makeup.

However, those factors can also be transformed into distinct advantages. Could Maria Bartiromo have broken into the alpha-male territory of Wall Street television commentary had she not been so different? Non–Barbie doll Sarah Palin came out of nowhere to command attention. Rupert Murdoch's contrarian business persona couldn't be missed. Clearly, Barack Obama leveraged his racial heritage, although very deftly. Talk show host Ellen DeGeneres seems to have become successful in incorporating her lesbian identity into her zany image.

In the current marketplace, career experts as well as employers, customers, and clients are telling job candidates, sales representatives, professional-services firms, and entrepreneurs that they want to see "something different." The trick is to position and package that difference or otherness in a way that doesn't make decision makers uncomfortable.

One entrepreneur, who prides herself on her ability to devise out-of-the-box solutions, invested nearly $30,000 (which she borrowed) in the best of hairstyles, makeup, suits, shoes, jewelry, writing folders, pens, and attaché cases. That sends a message of her success to businesspeople, as well as her understanding of the traditional rules of the game. That message helps them feel safe working with her ideas.

TAKEAWAYS

- Talk is never cheap. Its value is increasing rapidly in this digital era.
- What comes out of our mouths, as well as what we transmit through the second and third languages of body mannerisms and facial expressions, sends messages. From those, listeners infer information about the speaker's integrity, expertise, education, confidence, social class, worldview, and more.
- Being perceived as "different" or "the other" can influence what, and how, listeners hear what speakers say. Those perceptions can be transformed into advantages.
- Shrewd professionals treat all public discourse as strategic. They err on the side of caution. They offset that guardedness by employing stock phrases, body language, and facial expressions that serve to create connections with others.
- Self-consciousness is the kiss of death in public speaking.
- The most important advice: Know the audience.
- There are elements in a speaking situation one can't control. The best-case scenario is simply not coming out looking bad.
- Coaching helps and sometimes is necessary, such as when giving testimony in court and before congressional committees.

CHAPTER

18

BYLINED MATERIAL—IN ALL MEDIA

"If there's a 'trick' to writing bylined material that gets published, read, and resonates, it's to develop what I call a 'journalistic mind.'"

—Joe Pisani

....

PRINT, DIGITAL, AUDIO, AND VISUAL. All these media are now perfect homes for bylined opinion-editorials (op-eds), articles, books (print and electronic), letters to the editor, blog posts, tweets, comments on digital sites, video scripts, podcasts, and more.

"Bylined" is an insider term in the field of communications for using "I." And it's that "I," or the first-person voice, that gives bylined material its power. In some situations, the literal "I" might not appear in the actual op-ed or be used in a podcast. The author or speaker uses the third person. But given the genre of bylined pieces, it is implicitly understood that this is the opinion—and it should be a strong one—of the person whose name is on it. This is not a company opining. This is not a nonprofit. This is not the government. These are human beings putting themselves out there.

That is why the bylined approach is so influential. The format is *me-to-you.* That's special. That's intimate. That puts an individual's unique voice on the message. That allows for idiosyncratic stylistics. Most important, it gives the author total control over the message. If the author is employing a ghostwriter, then that scribe must function as a doppelgänger and express the voice of the author.

The good news is that this niche has been expanding rapidly because of digital technology. For years, the options for this sort of self-expression were limited. The game was essentially in print publishing, and it was highly competitive. Print, unlike the Web, has a finite amount of space, at least for that day, week, or month. As a result, public relations pros who were able to place their clients' op-eds in the *Wall Street Journal* or have book proposals accepted by an agent were heroes. In fact, that's how brand names were built among the leaders in the field of communications for years. As for other media, the use of video or audio for first-person material historically required high cost and special training. Consequently, they were underutilized.

Currently, there are more options, with lower costs. Because so many people around the world are media savvy, most only require minimal coaching. Think Joe the Plumber. Yet this first-person category remains a difficult field to master. That's the bad news.

Too many op-eds are ignored by editors. The lion's share of book ideas don't get published. Books that do get published all too often sell a mere 5,000 copies. Blogs are abandoned because of low readership. The chief executive officer discussing corporate changes on the video feed doesn't resonate with employees.

One reason for the failure is that all communications are in transition. All have been turned on their ear by the Internet. For example, the conversational tone of digital media has made statesmanlike prose or even any formality largely an anachronism. Yet authors and their PR representatives are submitting to *BusinessWeek* op-eds penned in high corporatese. What's expected is conversational prose: plain-speaking, chatty, accessible. Anything more buttoned-down or dense raises a red flag that one might be trying to hide something. Many business professionals can't adjust their tone. Those include first-person writers as well as their ghostwriters.

First-person communications cannot be disembodied. There must be a real human voice. And that voice must be distinctly the author's. Just because Harvard Business School professor Rosabeth Moss Kanter sells plenty of books doesn't mean others can or should sound like Kanter. Yes, it is a struggle to find one's own voice. Not everyone is willing to do that work. They are doomed not to be heard.

For a message to get any attention, it must be creating value or adding something fresh to the conversation. Boilerplate is not welcome. The world has too much to try to figure out. Yet, all some authors know how to do is serve up twice-fried platitudes in their communications. Strange, but the Organization Man still lives on in the twenty-first century.

In addition, the focus must be on an issue, not on the author or the company. An op-ed about healthcare, for example, must be on a pressing matter in patient care, not about the fine leadership of the president of a hospital or the hospital's excellent track record in the field. The effective political blog post must be about the need for transparency in state government, not an obvious or even subtle endorsement of a particular candidate. This is a strategy that works via indirectness.

Sure, it's a free country. The author may certainly be blatantly self-promoting about a company or a candidate in bylined material. But such an article is unlikely to be accepted by any credible media or, if put out there on the author's own digital, video, or audio vehicle, to have impact. In fact, the author is open to ridicule or risks becoming irrelevant in the conversation about important issues.

Another problem—and one that's not unique or new to digital media—is that sometimes the author, public relations pro, or ghostwriter doesn't do his or her homework. In the bylined niche, no one size fits all, nor should it. Effective communicators, be they Lee Iacocca, Barack Obama, or Nassim Nicholas Taleb (former trader turned philosopher and author of *The Black Swan: The Impact of the Highly Improbable*), drill down or have their team dig for information and insight about the region of the country, the city or town, the specific problems and opportunities in that area, and what's on the mind of the people they are addressing. In addition, they deconstruct the DNA of the particular publication, radio broadcast or podcast, or the digital community in which a blog has influence. Do anything less and the tone and content will scream "Carpetbagger!" and/or "He doesn't care about us."

Digital technology creates the expectation of interactivity. The one-way medium of television may attempt to simulate that interactivity with audience voting, viewer call-ins, and online tie-ins such as blogs. However, those add-ons are not adequate, which is why television is declining. The more the feedback mechanism is built into the vehicle for communications, the more potential for the message to resonate. Consider the Barack Obama game-changing presidential campaign.

Team Obama established the social media site My.BarackObama.com. That was a tool of empowerment. As Internet expert Don Tapscott, author of *Growing Up Digital*, notes, those wanting Obama to be America's next president could use the site as a platform "to build support, hold rallies, and raise money. Users are invited to post blogs, get into groups, meet people in the neighborhood, and track the money they're raising." Authors have to configure mechanisms for the same spirit of interactivity.

That's just an overview of pitfalls. But there are specific guidelines for boosting the odds of effectiveness with bylined material. Some of the advice that follows is operational know-how from old media and some of it comes from recent experience out there in cyberspace.

TRICK OF THE JOURNALISTIC MIND

Former reporter and newsroom managing editor Joe Pisani sees a "journalistic mind" as a bulletproof way to conceive, write, and find a home for just about any bylined material. Now a principal with The Dilenschneider Group, Pisani breaks down that mind-set into eight steps:

1. Be curious. Curiosity can turn up different angles. Angles make a topic interesting. That's what editors and agents demand. They have to, if they want to keep their jobs.
2. Know the audience on that particular day in their lives. Given the volatility in the world, the audience's concerns might change day to day or hour to hour.
3. Seek to render a public service, not promote anything. In cyberspace, self-serving material gets one flamed.
4. Simplify. Currently, all generations, not only the Millennials, have a reduced attention span.
5. Be accurate. Fact-check, even if you are blogging.
6. Be brief. That short attention span again.
7. Demonstrate integrity. The nation is hungry for evidence of character.
8. Tell stories or anecdotes. One of mankind's most primitive needs is for narratives to make sense of what is happening around us.

Over the years, Pisani has been most successful in his mission of educating the public about alcoholism through his first-person stories about his father's recovery from the disease through

Alcoholics Anonymous. He learned through trial-and-error. "When I wrote columns dealing with the facts about alcoholism," says Pisani, "there was little response. Then I started recounting my experiences with my father, and readers told me how I had changed their lives."

HARD SELLS

Every field has its hard sells. Bylined material is no exception. There are several tough nuts to crack.

One is placing first-person material in top-tier media, both print and online. Since many print publications also have different online versions, it may be easier to get into the online edition, but it's never easy.

What can make the submission more attractive to the editor? Here are some tips:

- Approach the editor or publisher with an idea, not the finished op-ed or article. In communications, that's called a "query." That allows the internal powers-that-be to regard the idea as theirs. From then on, the author takes on the role of implementing that idea. (Note: It's job number-one to establish relationships with members of the media, mainstream and digital.)
- In pitching any idea, briefly explain why it is helpful to readers and why the author is uniquely suited to comment. If the author published a book on the topic, FedEx a copy of it to the editor.
- Use topical positioning and packaging. It's probably shrewd to never submit anything without a current news peg on which to hang the subject.
- Use a catchy title and provocative opening paragraph—they are winners.
- Use enough argument or documentation to support a point of view. Too much will bleed into boring.

- Use recognizable analogies that aren't already clichés.
- Offer to revise, if necessary.

Another type of hard sell is getting, keeping, and increasing attention on the Internet. It's a dogfight. And those who have been online for any length of time say it's life in dog years.

Although one billion people have access to the Web, they are highly fragmented. Simultaneously, more sites are started daily. In addition, there's that issue of short attention span to factor in. Gawker.com was hot and then it was not. Here are recommendations for digital influence:

- Operate within a niche. Communities cluster around niches. If the niche gets too broad, cut it back to its initial focus and start other sites for the other topics.
- Make content provocative. The Web is communications on steroids.
- Use catchy headlines, brand names, topical references, popular keywords, and links to mainstream content, such as coverage in the *New York Times*. That attracts search engine pickup and links from other sites.
- Post often—every day, if possible.
- Analyze traffic every few hours, doing more of what is working.
- Use multimedia or include links to other kinds of sites with multimedia.
- Encourage relationships with the heavy hitters in the niche. That could bring links from them.

A third form of hard sell is the business of books. And it is a business since publishing a book is still the price of entry into many professions. These days, the traditional book publishing business is imploding. The model is broken and, as yet, no one has fixed it. Therefore, it is more difficult for a first-time author to find an agent or a publisher.

Here are the three options for having a book credit on one's resume and promotional literature:

1. *Conventional agent/publisher route.* Because it's sometimes difficult for a first-time author to get an agent, the most likely way in is to ask around your network of contacts for those who have published books. Ask their permission to approach their agent/publisher and to use their names. If that works, the author or the ghostwriter will probably be asked to prepare a few pages of a summary on the topic. Remember, books are a business. The next step would be a full-length book proposal. If the proposal is accepted, there could be a small advance. The process from acceptance to the book actually being distributed could take a year or more. If there is urgency, this is not the way to go.
2. *Self-publish using a full-service vendor.* This is the quicker and guaranteed approach. Self-publishing businesses such as iUniverse.com are equipped to handle the main tasks such as copyrighting, proofreading, printing, and distribution into bookstores and libraries. They charge a fee. That fee depends on the level of service, but usually doesn't exceed about $1,000. There are less expensive packages. Should the book take off, a traditional publishing house might pick it up.
3. *Self-publish an e-book.* This kind of project can be composed on a computer in Microsoft Word and distributed in the form of a PDF file. For a professional-looking book, a layout artist can be brought into the loop. Copyright can be done through Library of Congress forms downloadable on the Internet. The book can be distributed both electronically and as a hard copy. Again, if the book takes off, a conventional publisher might pick it up.

In all three options, the marketing is the author's responsibility—and expense. Only best sellers get marketing support from traditional publishing houses. Fortunately, digital technology makes marketing less of an ordeal and less expensive.

Pitching the book to online niche communities that have some relationship to the topic is probably the most effective marketing tactic. Actually, that's becoming standard. Off-line, there are trade and professional associations that deal with the subject matter of the book. They are excellent third-party allies in the promotion effort. They might put a blurb about the book on their website, invite the author to speak at events for association members, or review the book in their newsletter.

CONTROLLING THE MESSAGE

A bylined strategy establishes a platform for a message. That platform could have multiple parts, ranging from op-eds in *Forbes* to a series of books authored by third parties. That provides initial control. Next, how does the author maintain or increase control once the message is bouncing around in different formats, including print and digital media, and possibly video and audio? Here are the "must-dos":

- Monitor key media for what is being said about your work. Not everything can be monitored, of course. If something serious occurs, the author will know soon enough.
- Enlist third parties who can lend support in the event of an attack on your work. Yes, that means a generic crisis communications plan should be put in place beforehand.
- Have your own digital site set up and running beforehand too, so you can use it, if necessary, to respond to negative attacks.
- Evaluate the nature of any criticism or attack. In most cases, not responding is the best way of reacting.
- If the situation escalates, then respond on your own site or sites. Shut off the comment section of those sites. Call in third parties.
- When wrong, admit it. When right, say just that in human-speak. All statements should have a conversational tone. *Never use corporatese, legalese, or VIPese.*
- Don't rush to comment to the media. Interviews with mainstream media are a judgment call. It is not necessary to comment. A way to dodge that bullet is not to be available or to have the staff inform the media the author is traveling. One has no control about what other media will do with one's statement. Avoid a blanket "no comment."

- Know the legalities. If libel or defamation seems to be involved, threatening a lawsuit or actually filing one might swiftly end the episode. This is an underutilized tactic, but highly effective.

REINFORCING THE MESSAGE

In a digital world, usually several messages are tried out or test-marketed on a small scale. Those mini-rollouts can use all kinds of media mixes—old and new. Soon enough, one message will stand out. That one message has to be reinforced. That's always been the case.

Take this example: There is an urgent need for loving foster homes for adolescents. That message has to be communicated over and over again, and in varied formats. For example, if you can get an op-ed on the subject published in the *Washington Post*, then there should be a link to that on a blog and a riveting discussion on a podcast. Bookings on top TV talk shows might open up. If not, then the author can go the affiliate route, using the *Washington Post* op-ed as bait. The point is: A message that isn't reinforced is a message that isn't being controlled.

TAKEAWAYS

- The "I" is a powerful messaging tool.
- Develop a distinct voice (not easy).
- Think like a journalist, not like an advocate or promoter.
- Create a spirit of community, including building in a mechanism for interactivity.
- Be prepared for hard sells.
- Control the message, especially when under attack.
- Reinforce messages that resonate.

CHAPTER

MARKET RESEARCH

"The future will be increasingly less predictable."

—Nassim Nicholas Taleb

ACROSS ALL DISCIPLINES, financial markets expert Nassim Nicholas Taleb has been blowing up traditional mind-sets. In a best-selling book he has put forth his "Black Swan" proposition: 1) Life is full of developments that could not be predicted, and 2) those developments tend to also change the world in unpredictable ways. More and more leaders and people in the trenches are buying what Taleb is saying. Consider the way the Internet played out. It wasn't anticipated. It revolutionized all institutions. And everyone is still reeling from the impact, thirteen years after its broad availability.

In *The Black Swan: The Impact of the Highly Improbable*, Taleb simply states: "The future will be increasingly less predictable." For that reason, business research, and how it is to be effectively applied, is being rethought in a growing number of circles. This chapter discusses the evolution in how market research is viewed and used, and presents efficient and productive ways to go about doing such research or surveys. The chapter is based on the assumption that scientific inquiry is no longer regarded as sacred or even entirely reliable. Recall that the failed New Coke introduction was launched after conducting supposed thorough research.

CHANGING PERSPECTIVES

Perspectives toward research have been undergoing a sea change. One factor accounting for this transformation, and it's a major one, is the growing realization that what exists today, whether an attitude, a career path, or a company, might not exist tomorrow. Furthermore, insight into those entities might not shed any light on what will unfold tomorrow. In the world of the Black Swan, the past isn't necessarily prologue or even relevant.

That said, in an era of scarce resources, how much should be invested in any kind of research? A looming image is the executive who has the Midas touch, thanks to a golden gut instinct or intuitive decision-making abilities. That's the myth. The reality is that there is usually plenty of high-priced research underpinning the executive's stellar performance.

In the real world, too, a budget-strapped organization might likely first search secondary sources rather than summarily commissioning its own unique study. Major secondary research sources include the Institute for Public Relations (www.instituteforpr.com), the U.S. Census Bureau (www.census.gov), and the National Opinion Research Center at the University of Chicago (www.norc.uchicago.edu), among many others. A few decades ago, not having custom-made research could negate the credibility of a proposal or presentation. Fortunately, times have changed.

A second factor is the plummeting trust in research methodologies and agendas. Flawed research studies are now exposed routinely in the media. They cover the alleged shortcuts or downright fraud in some commercial research projects, such as those underwritten by pharmaceutical companies and the errors and outright misstatements that get by peer review in some scientific journals.

This credibility problem has become so pervasive that some attorneys advocate that, when scientific evidence is presented in jury trials, it become mandatory to provide the raw data along with a description of the methodologies used to acquire the evidence. In the summer 2008 issue of *Expert Alert*, Jones Day law firm partner Laura Ellsworth argues that "litigators seeking truth from scientists should be able to get it from examining the same source as the scientists—the actual data." The scientific method has mutated from a revered process to something open to corruption in ways that laypeople cannot easily discern.

The third factor is the push for a return to common sense. It was erudite mathematical formulas from market quants that helped get the global economy in such difficulty. All those ingenious models taught in the best business schools eventually did not preserve profitability for the world's major corporations. Society seems more inclined today to follow the approach of the Sage of Omaha, Warren Buffett. He refuses to deal with what he doesn't understand.

A fourth factor is the reemergence of the culture of romanticism, along with an embrace of mysticism; that is, accepting what isn't visible and what can't be empirically proved. As society becomes more high tech, ironically, this belief in the otherworldly will probably increase. Some researchers in spiritual matters are developing tools to investigate the impact of forces such as prayer on bodies and brains. Meanwhile, what can't be proved often sells like hotcakes.

TYPES OF RESEARCH

Clearly, perceptions of research have evolved from blind trust to caution. The amount of money to spend on research, the degree of reliance on research findings, and what aspects of a topic, development, or forecast should be investigated are all questions being explored.

Yet, according to the Marist Institute for Public Opinion (MIPO), organizations and individuals still demand "research be done." Headed by Director Lee M. Miringoff, MIPO conducts both quantitative, full-service, and omnibus research. This is different from what's known as qualitative research. One difference is the application of the rules or laws of probability to measure and compute results. As the term *quantitative research* indicates, the focus is on numbers and how reliable they are.

The cost of the full quantitative service could range from $20,000 to $100,000. The research can be conducted in person; over the phone; through snail mail, e-mail, or fax; and via call-ins. It can be formatted as an open-ended survey, a highly specific survey, or a poll.

It is important to note the negative side of this kind of research. It's called a "push poll." Ethical research firms won't take on these kinds of assignments. In a push poll, the questions are constructed to plant certain assumptions, questions, or facts in the minds of those interviewed. A typical push question in a political campaign might be, "Would you vote for Joe Smith if you found out he had been in a substance abuse facility three times?" Or "Would you vote for someone like Joe Smith, who raised taxes four times in three years?" Push polls can ferret out what issues are most damaging to the opposition. Their use, alas, is growing.

Qualitative research, on the other hand, involves generating and analyzing data impressionistically. That might be done through simple observation, focus groups, open-ended or narrow questions posed on blogs or microblogs, and conversations. The cost could be nothing or thousands of dollars.

Frequently, a full-service research effort includes both qualitative and quantitative techniques. A full-service survey includes:

- Initial brainstorming about what issues to explore. At the front end, qualitative methods, such as focus groups, may be used to discern what the right area of investigation should be.
- Study design. There are many ways to conduct the research.
- Sample selection—that is, establishing what population to survey or study. The sample is central; for example, it might be determined that the best sample would be females age 18–27 who have at least one year of college.
- Questionnaire construction. What questions to ask, in what order, and different methods of wording questions are tested out.
- Data collection.
- Data analysis.
- Report writing. A final report includes the raw data, its interpretation, and any implications to be made.
- Presentation to the client.

Omnibus research, or an omnibus survey, facilitates adding on a question or a number of questions to a full-service survey. The result is a larger study of issues related to the core question or questions. The advantage here is that the purchaser does not have to pay for a complete survey yet receives the same quantitative investigation that occurs in full service.

The cost of an omnibus survey can be relatively low, reports Walter K. Lindenmann, an expert in public relations research and author of the paper "Research Doesn't Have to Put You in the Poor House." The cost could be about $725 for the first closed-ended question. If there are multiple questions submitted, the cost keeps decreasing per question. The fifth question asked might be billed at about $525.

USES OF RESEARCH

Why is research, whatever form it might take, in such demand? MIPO gives five reasons, some of which may overlap. Research is needed to:

1. *Identify a market.* Would twenty-five-year-old, unmarried males be a target market for low-cost health insurance? Does the likelihood of those males buying insurance increase with certain variables, or a combination of them, such as income, living alone or with family of origin, or blue-collar/white-collar occupation?

2. *Test out messages.* Is a negative message, based on fear, more effective in marketing life insurance than a positive message about protecting loved ones?

3. *Determine brand attributes.* Should a soft drink be positioned as an energy or a relaxation beverage? Should it be marketed as an elite product, available in exclusive stores, or as a Main Street product that's sold everywhere? Which of these attributes are most important to the segment and should be highlighted?

4. *Create the right image.* Should the private school be perceived as preserving humanistic values and/or as an institution that prepares young people for a competitive professional marketplace?

5. *Pursue an issue in government relations.* In the political realm, research might be used for the selection of the right candidate to run for office, or to identify the key topics for the campaign, or to reach and organize constituencies, make a course correction, and fund-raise for reelection.

The key guideline is this: Never commission or conduct research if it can't be applied effectively in actionable ways. Research is never an end in itself. Even universities, which regularly publish research, usually do so as a profit center or to enhance branding and name recognition. Research consumes resources, even if the organization decides to do it itself, using inexpensive, secondary sources.

Before deciding to commission or conduct research, ask yourself these questions:

- How will this research be applied in an actionable way? No research should be destined to sit on a shelf.
- How much is already known? It costs money and slows down a project to reinvent the wheel.
- Is research a way to mask indecision and inaction? The metabolism of the professional world has been speeded up. Not acting entails added competitive risk.
- Are there other ways the organization can leverage research, such as using the findings in promotional materials or providing it as a freebie to members?

ENCOURAGING PARTICIPATION

Why do people agree to take part in research surveys? There are many incentives. However, astute researchers are aware that the appropriate incentives must be provided in order to encourage the right population to respond. Consider an animal rescue organization that wants to explore what will motivate non–animal lovers to donate. It might provide the incentive of sponsoring legislation that restricts the number of pets in a household. The organization would then ask those people it interviews how that bill should be framed.

Some of the proven incentives in political research are offering a sense of belonging, making a difference, being heard, and even assuming the role of leader or organizer. In business research, there could be the appeal of free merchandise or cash, a chance to win a major prize or to appear in a commercial, or the incentive might be improving the environment or creating jobs.

DO-IT-YOURSELF RESEARCH

In addition to just paying attention to one's environment, making some hypotheses, and then testing them out, there are myriad ways to conduct research on one's own. Here are some possible approaches, based on methods that have been utilized successfully in the past by others:

- Come up with an incentive for ten women to come to a specified house and wash their hair with Shampoo Y. Generate a conversation between the facilitator and the women and among the women themselves about the shampoo's attributes. Focus on the product's aroma, hand feel, head feel, results in terms of sheen, color enhancement, volume fullness, cleanliness, and get everyone's impressions on price points. This is a rudimentary focus group. More sophisticated models would be to set up a hidden viewing window and to write up most comments. A formal report would be made about the statements, body language, and facial expressions of each member of the group, with interpretations provided.
- Conduct a just-in-time poll on a website or on several sites. This type of initiative is called *hyperdemocracy.* The question might be: Will the president's prime-time press conference help, hurt, or have no effect on his ability to sell his budget to Congress and Main Street? To encourage participation, voters can immediately view ongoing results. Later, a report on the poll and its implications can be posted on the site, as well as provided in press release form to other media.
- Ask for input from visitors to a website and via links to other websites. When a career counselor was writing her book for Millennials on getting that first job, she put out a call for help. On her own blog and microblog she asked what new entries to the world of work needed to know. She asked other sites to also post this query. More than 20,000 responses came in.

- Make the first stop secondary data. There's a gold mine of information out there for those who know what to do with it. The U.S. Commerce Department has a 1,000-page guide called the "Statistical Abstract of the United States." In this instance, the government is really there to be helpful. Plugging diverse keywords related to a topic into search engines will also turn up published and unpublished dissertations, white papers, court documents, web seminars, and YouTube videos. The only requirement is the patience to sort through all the material.
- Barter with a freelancer in research. How the work is divvied up depends on skill sets. The organization can do its own rudimentary surveying and turn the data over to a research student for tabulation. In return, the student might receive free lodging or use of commercial office space.
- Conduct Internet polls using low-cost software. This is how Toby Bloomberg, who operates Atlanta-based Bloomberg Marketing, gathered information before starting an e-business. By logging into sites such as InsightExpress (www.insightexpress.com) and Zoomerang (www.zoomerang.com), she found survey templates to use to create her online questionnaire. Costs here can range from a few hundred dollars to about $1,000.
- Pass out samples and ask for feedback. The more sophisticated version of this approach is providing equipment, products, or services for a certain period and then asking about the pros and cons and for recommendations for improvement.
- Use performance art as a unique pull force. Putting on a good show builds a sense of obligation, so audiences willingly answer questions or try out products and services. This approach is underutilized by large companies even though it can be a good way to gain exposure for the brand. So put on free puppet shows, if your market segments include children or senior citizens, to gain their feedback.
- Simply request human being to human being input. It may sound primitive, but it is effective. Increasingly, entrepreneurs, the unemployed, and those considering professional school are picking up the phone or creating an e-mail blast to get some

input. It could be as formal as asking, "Would you just take a quick look at this logo?" or it can be an informal inquiry, such as: "Is law school a big mistake?"

TRIAL-AND-ERROR

Research is the first step in a process. What emerges can be frustrating trial-and-error that might require even more research. Or the organization might discover it has been investigating the wrong variable in the initial research. For instance, a real estate firm conducted a survey about price point and marketability when what was actually on potential homebuyers' minds was tax credits.

TAKEAWAYS

- Volatility and an increasing inability to predict the future are game-changers in the discipline of research.
- Scandals, return to common sense, and the new romanticism have raised skepticism about blind trust in science.
- Cost and immediate applicability are what organizations need to make priorities. Research is a means, never an end.
- The two major categories of the discipline are quantitative research, which uses rules of probability, and qualitative research, which relies on human observation and judgment.
- According to the MIPO, there are five core reasons for research: identifying a market, testing a message, determining brand attributes, developing an image, and dealing with issues and decisions in government relations.
- There are myriad forms of do-it-yourself research.
- Research is only the first step in a process of trial-and-error in applying the findings. That exercise may be frustrating and demand additional or even completely new research.

AFTERWORD

AS I WRITE, the Chrysler Corporation and General Motors have both recently emerged from bankruptcies that few would have thought possible a scant number of years ago. These developments help answer why the book you are holding is important—that is, why we should care about public relations.

Not long ago, General Motors was the nation's corporate colossus. Its cars and trucks were everywhere, and its power and influence seemed permanent parts of American life. The possibility that it would one day accept tens of billions of dollars in government loans to stay afloat, and even then sink into insolvency, was simply unthinkable. But nothing is impossible anymore.

My point is that change, often rapid and sometimes shocking, is an unavoidable fact of modern life, and we all must be prepared for it. Much of this preparation, whether we work for an organization or on our own, has to do with public relations of the kind described in this book—how we present ourselves to the world; how we deliver our message; and how we reach the right audiences, whether digitally or through older, more traditional channels.

You never know when you are going to need a friend—whether a member of Congress, a bishop, a professor, or simply an unbiased observer with the capacity to shape events and influence opinions. As any of the executives at GM can now testify, even when times are prosperous and one is riding high, it's smart to maintain open lines of communication, cultivate contacts, and burnish your reputation. In other words, it's always wise to practice sound public relations.

How we go about effectively communicating with one another is a constantly evolving business. Gutenberg's printing press launched one revolution back in the fifteenth century. The rise of mass circulation newspapers in the nineteenth century triggered the next big development. Then came radio, television, the Internet, handheld devices—the pace of change now is astonishing, and there's no telling what is next to come.

Yet, the basics of sound and effective public relations remain the same—clarity, honesty, thoroughness, timeliness. All this is what this book is about, while it also reflects the adjustments you must make to fit your message into the latest delivery systems.

I've been a journalist all my career, which means I've been on the receiving end of a lot of the public relations profession's work. I know that, at their best, PR pros can perform a double service, increasing the flow of information to the public realm while helping their employers or clients get their stories told.

Public relations should be honorable and deserving work. How it can be is what this book is all about, and is why it is not only a useful guide, but also a valuable contribution to the ongoing dialogue between people who have a message to deliver and those who can benefit from receiving it.

—Marshall Loeb

APPENDIX

TACTICS FOR KEEPING UP DIGITALLY

- Key in a number of different terms and phrases as keywords at the various search engines (Google, Bing, Yahoo!, and others). To remain up-to-date on what's being posted on the Web about your organization, discipline, and the competition, try searches for these topics: monitoring the Internet, Internet monitoring services, digital reputation management, detecting cyber-bullying, flaming, digital damage control, digital crisis management, the top 100 sites in law/public relations/manufacturing/healthcare (or substitute another industry name). The search results will point you to current information, insights, services, and other resources for finding out what people are talking about on the Web.
- Identify what are the most influential digital sites in your profession or industry. Bookmark them and check them at least daily (update the list as necessary, too, since it might change over time). Influence doesn't have to correlate with prestige of the site or quality of content.
- Useful resources are available at the Berkman Center for Internet & Society at Harvard Law School—Http://cyber.law.harvard.edu/media/.
- Check out Amazon for relevant books coming on the market. That service provides book descriptions before actual publication dates, as well as book previews of most other books currently available.

- Read publications focused on technology, including *Technology Review* (published by MIT) and *Wired.* They usually post some free content online and sell subscriptions for the print copy.
- Form a user's group online and/or in salon fashion for discussion of the PR-related topics in this handbook. Insights from in-person salon discussions can be posted online.
- Join free digital groups on social networks such as LinkedIn, which particularly serves members in the business and professional worlds.
- Attend Internet seminars, conferences, and workshops in your own discipline. The investment is worth it and often tax deductible.
- Establish an interactive site and become an actual player. Put your site in the loop for receiving information. The Web has been called the "ultimate listening post."

NOTEWORTHY RESOURCES

Media Blogs

All Things Digital (*Wall Street Journal*).

John Bartelle's Searchblog—thoughts on the intersection between search, media, technology, and more.

CyberJournalist—news and resource site that focuses on how the Internet, convergence, and new technologies are changing the media.

Huffington Post: Media—media news and opinions.

Mashable—the social media guide.

MediaFile (Reuters)—where media and technology meet.

MediaShift (PBS)—guide to the digital media revolution.

Social Media Today—the Web's best thinkers on social media and web 2.0.

Publishing 2.0.—the (r)evolution of media.

TechCrunch—weblog dedicated to profiling and reviewing new Internet products and companies in addition to profiling existing companies that are making an impact (commercial and/or cultural) on the new web space.

Internet Sites

iMedia Connection (www.imediaconnection.com)—connecting the marketing community.

The Industry Standard (www.thestandard.com)—news and analysis about the technologies that are changing people's lives and the ways in which companies do business.

Publications

Wired Magazine

Technology Review

Groundswell: Winning in a World Transformed by Social Technologies

INDEX

ABOUT THE AUTHOR

ROBERT L. DILENSCHNEIDER formed The Dilenschneider Group in October 1991. Growing rapidly, the firm soon attracted as clients many of our best-known domestic and foreign companies. He has since personally counseled numerous major corporations, professional groups, trade associations and educational institutions, assisting them in dealings with regulatory bodies, labor unions, consumer groups, and minorities, among others.

Experienced in a broad range of communications disciplines, Mr. Dilenschneider is now also frequently called upon by the media to provide commentary and strategic public relations insights on major news stories.

In addition to authoring eleven books, he has lectured before scores of professional organizations and colleges, including the University of Notre Dame, The Ohio State University, New York University, and The Harvard Business School.

Mr. Dilenschneider is a member of the Council on Foreign Relations, the U.S.–Japan Business Council, the Economic Clubs of New York and Chicago, the Florida Council of 100, the Public Relations Society of America, and the International Public Relations Association.

Robert L. Dilenschneider launched his career in public relations in 1967 shortly after receiving an MA in journalism from The Ohio State University and a BA from the University of Notre Dame.

Printed in the USA
CPSIA information can be obtained
at www.ICGtesting.com
JSHW051126020624
64117JS00004B/8